A Kindness Of Ravens

A Kindness
Of Ravens

Rhyd Wildermuth

GODS&RADICALS PRESS

First Printing 2015
This is the second printing

ISBN: 978-0-9969877-9-0
Published by Gods&Radicals Press
PO BOX 11850
Olympia, WA, 98508

Direct all inquiries to the above address,
or email us at
Distro@abeautifulresistance.com

Within

-To-

To you, who dare.
To you, who once dared.
To you, who will dare again….
…and again
…and again.

The Blackening

Almost three years ago now, everything broke around me. The great white tower spanning far into an endless sky would no longer go away, the laughing woman before the raging fire would not disappear.

I tried to make them go away, like you try to deny love or a toothache. "Narcotics cannot still the tooth..." said the haunted shut-in, and I tremble to think what she saw.

Everything exploded into meaning while everything of me crumbled into ruins, fast-forwarded decay, *solve* over minutes and seconds in a black fire. And then I started writing.

Here are some of those words for you, compiled and culled from that realm of backlit shadows, distilled from another year of meaningful madness, whispered from tongueless mouths crawling from the Cauldron of Annwn reeking of coal-dust, dried blood, raped mountains and leafless forests.

But this sounds dark, morbid even. My apologies. Hours and months tracing the paths the dead take to and from our world, listening for the swinging-open of gates no mortal can open will make you sound a bit morose. The dead are a bit intense.

7

The dead are hardly murderous, though—not like the living. A few days before I'm composing this introduction for you, there was a massacre of people in Paris, noticed particularly because some white European middle-class people died. Over a hundred stories ended there, another collection of tales joining the endless narrative of the tormented in every city in the world. We care a bit more about some of those, a lot less about others, and we never care much for the awful truths threading all those apparently unrelated deaths together.

I'll not pontificate; it's tiring, and never why you've read me anyway, and never why I ever put words to paper.

Why do I write, though?

Because I'm a horrible photographer, an unskilled painter, a graceless performance artist, a clumsy musician. Words are the only way I know how to show you what I'm seeing, what I hear, what is becoming, what is going away, and what everything means.

I'm lying. Actually, I'm trying to initiate revolutionaries into the madness of the poets and the wisdom of the dead.

In the preface to my last compilation, *Your Face is A Forest*, I wrote:

"All I know is this: meaning is what connects you to others, connects us to the stars and the graves, to the light and soil, to the cities and the streams, to what we see and what we cannot see."

I forgot to mention the Dead, it seems. I'll not make that mistake this time.

Our modern madness is the fear of death, the terror of decay, capitalism's anxiety about its inevitable demise inhabiting our own consumption. Everything's to prolong lives whose meaning has been stretched thin, doled out and delivered from Markets in which we are mere passive participants, anesthetized patients awaiting some chirugic intervention which might finally infuse us with the meaning we've lost.

Meantime, our world's dying. I don't say "the earth," because it'll do just fine—probably better—without us. What bits of the natural world that's still on our side is having an awful time of it, what still wants us around is having serious doubts, and what's trying to keep us alive is getting awfully exhausted.

"Western Civilization" is going away, which is quite the relief, but the priests of Capital and Authority who've tended its altars for the last three hundred years are sharpening their ritual blades, aware of an old truth every brutal Empire recalls in its dying days. When none of the usual offerings suffice, there's always the human, and some dark things we wisely put to slumber are awakening to the sounds of their oblations.

Meantime, the gods we pushed away, sent back into the sea or under mountain, haven't lain idle. You might call them by the names I call them, The Raven King, the Liberator, the Lady of The Forge, the Crown of the North, the Bent White One. Or you might just call them revolution.

A massing of crows is called a Murder, a massing of ravens is an Unkindness. That's nonsense, of course. Like the modern propaganda against the Dead, they've been smeared unfairly, no doubt to warn against the very alliances we need most.

The dead whom I see most often, whom I call "The Revolutionary Dead," wear the feathers of corvids. Bards were said to wear cloaks of raven feathers, and some of these dead are bards, so I leave those who haven't put this book back on a shelf by this point to draw their own conclusions about the initiatory current here.

But they are most certainly quite kind.

This collection will hopefully help you meet the dead. Or it may lead you, as I've been led, to a fierce magic whose snarling howls at the moon drown out the timid chants to gossamer-gowned goddesses, asking not for blessings, but for fire to wield against our oppressors. It's equally for the witchpunx as the intellectuals, but more for the poor than ever for the rich.

I've arranged the writing in *A Kindness of Ravens* into four sections which, at least to me, describe best the blind initiatory path I've stumbled along since encountering the Raven King. The sections also loosely follow Jung's (likely mis-) reading of the Alchemical journey as seen in Marguerite Yourcernar's novel, *The Abyss*. As things often go, I did not notice such a parallel until arranging the works, nor the (now hilarious) inclusion of the quartet of fragments—written just before an awfully brutal initiation—entitled Love Notes From The Abyss.

If I've done my work correctly, you may find some gates opened to you. That's always really been the point of any of this.

The first section, **The City At The Gates of The Dead**, collects words on the Dead and our own destruction. Here's a bit of *nigredo*, and perhaps a bit of a warning for those who might, from a mere adolescent curiosity or "will-to-power," rattle the gates from our side.

What Wants Us Gone describes, in shattered blood-soaked glass, a suicide attempt 20 years ago. *What They Do Not Tell You* is a poem written after finding myself experiencing the death of someone long-dead, a revolutionary whose life drained un-mourned into significant soil.

Like most else I write, *Brighid in the Dumpster, Brân in the Bad Heroin* describes an actual event, and was written in response to an antagonist's assertion that I worship "small gods." *Maybe, Another Vein* is an Equinox meditation exploring Capital's insistence we can always innovate our way out of every crisis Capital creates.

The City at the Gates of the Dead is another meditation on the nightmare of capitalist civilisation with the vision of a Bard of Annwn woven through it. *After The Fire, Invisible* is a love poem...sort of.

The second, **She Sends A Flood Upon The World,** takes its title from a less-common translation of *The Chair of Ceridwen*. The popular reading's got Arianrhod sending a rainbow 'round the earth, as if she's Yahweh all apologetic. However, the sea-witches I've met thus far have all been about drowning. Here are pieces about overthrow of all that would rule, including the Ego. Several of these are essays which have gotten me some shade from other witch-folk. Learn to unweave hexes if you take this path.

Perceval and *Dahut At the Floodgates* are both anarchist challenges against those who—seeing the resurgence of the old powers and new magics—would dare set themselves as pontiff or king, and both made me quite a few enemies. *Awakening the Land* is an introduction to The Raven King and the mysteries of the uprising land. *Delaying The Flight* is another love poem. *The Roots of Our Resistance* was written originally for Gods&Radicals, an introduction to the way of an animist understanding of place can inform our resistance to gentrification and capitalist displacement. *Putting Out* is a narrative about sex-work and the so-called Sharing Economy, placing both within the framework of Silvia Federici's Anarcho-Feminist Marxism. And *The Multitude&The Myriad* assaults our conceptions of binary gender and binary Deity through the anarchist theory of Michael Hardt and Antonio Negri.

Until The Forest Becomes The World begins with *The Land Across The Waters,* a devotional poem describing my experience in a ritual to The Mothers. The next series of pieces are my pilgrimage journals from Winter, 2014. I was selected to be inside Newgrange for Midwinter Solstice, and the story as to how that happened still awes me. A friend saw visions of me in Dublin several times in one day (I'd never been there before). He went to Newgrange the next day and entered my name into the pool of almost 40,000 applicants for 50 slots for Winter Solstice. I still shake my head in wonder that I was selected. The story is told again in *The Tomb of the Atheist*. This section ends with *The DisEnchanted Kingdom*, a Wildean fairytale about Capital and Magic and toilet paper.

The final section, **The Forest That Will Be**, compiles some of my more esoteric and political writing with a hope towards showing how only, without a revolutionary current within Paganism, Witchcraft, and the other magical traditions, it's all just fantasy role play, useless in the face of a dying world. It's also mostly about love.

Awaiting Night's Final Falling is a dream. *All That is Without You* is about love and madness, written just before another initiation. *If You'll Not Die Antinous* and *Fire in Winter* are both poems that have outlasted the lovers for whom they were written.

What Do They Mean? is the text of a speech prepared for Many Gods West, and outlines a theory of meaning. The speech was well received, though I'm sure I didn't use my notes. *The Forest That Will Be* is an almost reluctant defense against anti-civilisationist thinking derived from a night at a gay bar on Samhain.

Though the magic of a writer is to weave meaning, no one ever weaves alone. The words of the dead and the echoes of the unborn, shadows of ancient forests and seeds not yet planted—nothing is ever fully written, and it all unfolds into the now. What you make of these pages is not up to me any longer, and maybe never was. Still, it's my hope you find gates opened which seemed forever closed, and learn to open more for the rest of us.

Be always well.
Occupied Duwamish Territory
Winter, 2016

The City At
The Gates Of
The Dead

A few years ago I stood with a man in another place on a blasted hillside. He looked like me, but wasn't me. We knew each other from another time, the past or future—I don't know.

He showed me the city at the gates of the dead, the world-city, all we are and all we've become and all we will be.
And then he showed me its destruction.

What I remember most was his face below a black hood. His expression was urgent and familiar, stern and kind—a lost brother, a dead lover whose arms I'd not yet felt around mine.
He was a bard of the Raven King, as I would one day become. We shared the same blood, coursing hot in the dark places none see. Bring our life to light, and it is lost, spilled out forever, only to return in other forms, but never again as us.

We stood together, watching the desolation wrought upon the city at the gates of the dead, silently. I breathed; he did not.

"You understand?" he asked me.

I told him I did.

I lied.

Love Notes From
The Abyss, I

The closer the blade gets to your heart,
the more you must not back away.

The faster the crow's beak flies toward your eyes,
the more you must not flinch.

The hotter and more intolerable the flames,
the more resolute you must stand.

You are not being harmed.

You are being healed.

What Wants
Us Gone

I don't want to write about this. My whole soul screams against it, like when my quads scream against riding on a hard-gear up a Seattle hill, or my arms groan agonised protest against another set of bicep curls.

I don't want to write about this, like when I don't want to meet new people, don't want to get out of bed some mornings.

Like when my heart refuses to let itself be loved by someone unfamiliar to it, or my mind aches upon reading something more complicated than it prefers to handle.

I don't want to write about this, but I will.

I.

I remember staring at the pavement below, crying. My hands were slippery with blood, the palms pierced with bits of glass. It took a long time to remove those.

It was chill. I was shaking, drunk.

I was 20, too young to drink, but had drank half a bottle of whiskey. I still can't even handle more than a shot of the stuff; two beers and I'm sloshed...I have trouble believing I'd drank so much of that shit, but I had.

It was the thing to do, I guess. I had someone else buy it for me. I'd never had the stuff before–I'd only three or four times even had alcohol, and I hated it.

I didn't smoke yet, but had gotten that same friend to buy me a pack of cigarettes. I smoked half of them. That hurt later.

Everything hurt later. Everything hurt then, too.

Something was in me, I guess. Some idea that's never fully left, which is also a process that has never fully ended, and a presence never exorcised. There's little difference between the three; a god's an idea, and a process, and a presence. Some insist only the first, some allow the second, few ever admit to the third.

But...this wasn't a god. None would give such a thing worship, except perhaps the most foulest of humans, and even then they'd be consumed by its hunger long before it had a chance to spread its disgusting gospel.

What it was, I still don't know, but I see it sometimes, right at the moment I least want to see it, right at the moment I've taken off every piece of armor I've donned to protect myself from it.

II.

I'd punched through a window with my fists. Windows don't shatter like you'd think they do when you punch through them. You have to punch a few times, shredding your knuckles each time. And even then you can't punch any longer—you have to pull the rest from the frame with your blood-slicked fingers.

I crawled through the frame onto the short ledge outside. Shards pierced my knees as I knelt surging pain into my body like no other. I almost lost my balance, which would have foiled my plan.

I sat in the glass, crying. I picked up the shards, blood-smeared. They made good blades, crystalline, fragile, like bits of ice off a frozen lake-shore, cold. Sharp. With them I sliced into my skin, enacting a ritual that felt pre-scripted, written long before we ever walked the earth.

What went through my head, I don't remember. I couldn't breathe; something was pressing there, crushing my lungs, pulling the air from my body. Like a "panic attack," or hyperventilation, except the feeling (and here's where things get crazy) was from without as well as within.

The "trigger" was a scenario of abandonment, but neither the scenario nor the trigger are quite as relevant as you think. We mythologise the human psyche like we mythologise our infections, our conditions, and our failures, all dark, injurious laments rather than epic strength and heroism. "Abandonment issues" one might say, dismissively, or as a shorthand for a slightly deeper "complex." But I, being the one who survived it, may call it what I like, name it as I saw it. I call it a haunting.

III.

When I was eight, growing up in Appalachia, I had a strange series of dreams and waking visions I still do not understand.

I once woke in the middle of the night with my nose touching the ceiling; turned around to see my body laying on my bed and panicked, finding myself back asleep.

I remember once sitting in a bath asking my cognitively-disabled (and later schizophrenic) mother what happened to all my siblings she drowned in the bathtub. Except it wasn't her who had drowned them, but another mother, and there'd been 5 or 6 of them. I was my mother's first. I'm sure it did my mother no good to hear those questions from me.

I remember most of all the long series of dreams after that. Eight days, I think it was, each night waking, staring out my window to see the man in a spaceship waiting for me. He'd take me inside and it was no longer spaceship at all, but a stone room, a monk's cell. He wore robes. He smiled sadly. He had me read strange writing in a book so he could "return to the stars."

The night I finished reading the book, he returned to the stars and I forgot what was in the book, though sometimes I wake remembering a page or two now.

A few years later is when my father started beating me. I remember it deeply; he'd whip me with his leather belt repeatedly, and then make up horrific rituals for it.

He'd make me go fetch his belt. One time he made me take his belt off of him before beating me.

The beatings were so bad I began to go into convulsions at random times, crying that I wanted to "go home." And both my parents would assure me I was home, but I knew better, because there was the woman who'd come to me as I slept and would hold me, a large Black woman, much bigger than anyone I'd ever seen, bigger still than anyone I've yet seen. She'd hold me really close and assure me that it was going to be okay later and I shouldn't worry, but I remember she'd cry when she held me.

I'm crying right now.

There was this other time when I was so terrified I thought I wouldn't survive and this guy came to me. He was with me, but a later me, and we were in Paris, and he told me that I'd be in Paris later (I didn't even know where Paris was at the time) so I should "hang on, okay?"

I did.

After my parents took me to counseling (probably state-mandated, I don't know), the beatings stopped. I remember asking my father in the car later what the counselor said, and he got really angry and said "she tol' me I cain't beat you wit' the belt." And I remember his anger about this, but at least he'd stopped, acting somehow shocked that such a thing could affect a kid.

IV.

I still don't want to write this, you know.

I'm sitting on that roof, on all that broken glass many stories up from the pavement. I'm terrified as I slice open the skin of my wrists. It takes a lot to get at a vein, you know, at least when you're drunk out of your mind and can't see for the tears and the blood in your eyes from where you'd cut your forehead pushing your body through that broken window.

I wanted it all to end, because I'd seen it again, that thing, that darkness, that haunting. I saw something that wants us gone, something that wants us destroyed.

It's the same thing you see on the streets, hanging around the piss-soaked homeless woman with necrotic skin infections. It's what you see in the after-image of the meth-addict scratching his face off.

It's what you see in the oil slick on a forest stream and the trash dumped off the side of a hill, but it's not quite the same there. I think sometimes there are different trenches in the same no-man's land, facing each other, two armies in an epic war, but few never know which side we're on.

I escaped much of that war in those hills. I was the only boy I knew who didn't get molested. Cousins, friends, neighbor boys all had stories, acted really strange and didn't want to be around certain men any longer. The one that haunts me the most is the kid from school I brought to sunday school as part of an attendance drive.

I won a trip to a chain restaurant in town for bringing the most friends; but one of the kids I brought never spoke to me again after my sunday school teacher pulled off my friend's pants to "check his underwear" in front of a room full of broken-toothed, mostly shoeless kids. And then that sunday school teacher gave him a ride home, and that friend never talked to me again.

Jesus loves you, by the way.

Me, though? Mostly unscathed. I'm pretty sure the man with the book from the stars had a lot to do with that, probably the same way I escaped brain cancer from the leaking nuclear power plant a few miles from our home, asthma or worse from burning coal in a wood-burning stove in a small house one long winter. Probably the same way I survived that autumnal suicide attempt a decade later, or avoided being driven off a bridge by my mother a few years later.

Maybe you already know this. My mother's schizophrenic, I raised my sisters mostly alone for much of my adolescence while working and going (sorta) to high school. That shit kinda fucks you up in some strange ways.

Mothers are our archetype for "goddess" usually, which is all fine and good for those who had mothers who weren't trying to kill their kids because demons were telling them to, or who gave entire paltry paychecks over to a megachurch to help them build a new building, or grabbed an intercom phone in a grocery store, hit the button, and told the assembled shoppers in her perpetual young-girl voice:

"Everybody accept Jesus Christ as your personal lord and savior because I have a bomb and am going to kill you all."

She was always particularly intent on doing the right thing, that woman. And as horrifying as that was at the time, I still find it also kinda funny.

V.

I tell you I don't want to write this shit?

This stuff haunts you, because you see someone who's supposed to be your sole guardian against the world disintegrate before your eyes, you hear your little sisters cry in fear about how "mom's talking to herself again" and then, worst-of-fucking-all, you find yourself pretty certain you're becoming like her when the darkness claws at your chest on a ledge as you're bleeding from both wrists.

Or later, too, when you can't get out of bed because your whole soul feels drained.

Or later, when you try to explain something you saw or think to someone you love and admire, someone you want to be loved and admired by, and they give you a blank stare like you just told them you saw a god or something.

And, of course, you've told them that, too.

Sometimes when I write about this, helpful people warn I'm encouraging people not to seek mental health help. It's strange to hear that, having woken up in a white padded room on a hard bench with both of my wrists wrapped in so much gauze I thought my fingers had been amputated. Also, it sucks to wake up restrained, by the way, almost as much as it sucks to be beaten up by a friend with a broom, or by cops when they finally arrived.

Nah, seriously. Go get treatment if you need it. There's shit that wants us gone.

What wants us gone? I…I don't really know.

I've seen the Burnt Ones. They're really terrifying, their skin crackling like thin layers of ash off charred wood, or flakes of blue-black coal. Not sure what they're on about, really, except they show up and warn you not to do something that's about to change your life, because you might not survive it.

What they don't tell you, of course, is that we survive everything until we don't. And that's just death, and that's hardly all that avoidable, eventually.

But really, the things you see in vision are benevolent compared to what you see with your eyes—if you look, anyway. Cops killing Black men, poisoned rivers, countries bombed to bits while people watch the aftermath on television while sitting down to dinner. No dark abyssal creature, no haunting being compares to a woman tripping a fleeing Syrian refugee to help the border police catch him, a well-known atheist arguing it was cool to arrest a Muslim boy who brought a clock to school, nor the nightmare of watching everyone around you stare at a little phone in their hand while there's a rainbow in the sky above you.

I'll take tea with an Archon or the restless dead any day over those people.

VI.

I told you I didn't want to write about this, but I knew how this would go. I knew I'd cry about half-way through writing this, and somewhere about word 1200, I'd go make tea, stare at the moon outside, come back to these words and remember why I write this stuff.

I write this stuff against what wants us gone, weaving the only magic I have full faith in, against that darkness others call "light" and "civilization." I write this stuff to exorcise what wants us gone, and to give you tapestries to keep you warm when the soul's winter comes. I write this stuff so you don't think you're fucking crazy. Because you're not. This other shit is. We're what makes this world bearable.

Two years ago, I'd just come down from an ancient druid mountain in France called Menez Hôm. and I guess 18 years ago, I was about to jump off a building.

The plan was simple. I'd get so drunk I couldn't feel any pain. I'd slash open the veins in both of my wrists. And then I'd throw myself off the roof. The combination of all of it would certainly work–if one didn't kill me, the other thing would, and I'd no longer have to worry about what wants us gone.

I'd also no longer have to worry about being thought crazy again. My mother's schizophrenia scared me, because it wasn't just babbling incoherence. She'd predict stuff that was about to happen. She'd read people's thoughts. She'd have visions.

My own depression, my own difference, terrified me, too. I remember when people found out I was gay and mostly fled from me. Or when I'd gotten suicidal at Christian college, got on meds, and then had the fact that I was taking anti-depressants used against me when I applied for an editor position with the college newspaper. "How can we know your job performance won't be affected?" they'd asked, and, well…

Fuck job performance. Fuck being the same. And fuck being terrified of what you see, and especially fuck apologizing for not being like everyone else.

VII.

They say trauma causes delusion.

"They" are right. And also very wrong.

Trauma, if anything, causes you to see differently. It's traumatic to watch someone get shot by a cop, or die of a condition they wouldn't die from it if they weren't poor. It's traumatic to watch a woman trip a Syrian refugee, it's traumatic to see a god.

It all makes you see things differently. And what you do with that difference determines whether you survive, whether you fight your government or become addicted to drugs or end up bleeding to death after jumping from a roof.

I see stuff differently, and that's why you're reading me. Sometimes I see the way you do. Sometimes I show you a way of seeing differently. Sometimes I just write pretty stuff, but this is hardly pretty.

Just as I was about to jump that day, 18 years ago, my friend showed up. I'm not sure why. Probably the friend who'd bought me the whiskey and cigarettes thought it was a bit bizarre and told him. Probably I'd said some stuff that gave them clues–I always think I'm more cryptic and closed-off than those who love me find me to be. I'm only ever fooling myself, anyway.

He shows up. Pulls me back through the window. I remember shouting "let me die" or some other ridiculous futile protest. It was all pretty futile by that point–I already knew I'd end up in Paris some day, and I hadn't been to Paris yet.

Trying to pull the pages out of a book to get to the end earlier doesn't work, not when the man-from-the-stars made you read that book when you were eight years old, or when the Black goddess told me it was gonna be okay and I'd see her again.

Beats the fuck out of me, he does—he and his brother. And then the cops come. They hurt pretty bad, by the way–don't fight them without friends, and not in one of those really rare moments they're actually trying to keep you alive.

And now I'm writing all this stuff to you, regardless of whether I wanted to or not. Like working out, or probably giving birth to a child, the pain's worth it afterward. Who wants a baby stuck inside them forever?

Who really wants us gone?

VIII.

People who know me personally tell me I'm one of the kindest people they know. It's one of the few compliments I'll ever accept from most people, most times, because it's the only thing I can say I've honestly decided to be. Because I've seen what wants us gone, what wanted me gone, and someone's gotta fight that.

And occasionally people will remark on the vividness of my visions, or how it seems incredible I see so many things so frequently. That one, I used to worry about, actually, because it made me wonder if they thought I were crazy, or delusional, or lying. Fear of being thought insane is unshakeable, if you've had the sort of mother I've had.

A skeptic might claim the visions I had as a child or the visions I have now are mental tricks to compensate for the trauma I experienced. There's no difference in my mind between such a position and those who claim

Syrian refugees should be made to go back home, or that Black men shot by police "had it coming."

No. I'm not crazy. I get to decide this, by the way—I'm the one who survived all that. I just look at trauma that others don't look at, and let it teach me to see differently.

I look at the way everyone's miserable with capitalism but tell themselves "it's the only option," and I see the trauma there and I learn to see what can be instead.

I look at the way homelessness and addiction and racism and poverty and dead forests aren't just unfortunate side-effects of the way we've set up civilization but the very requirements for the rest of us to have 'nice things,' and I learn to see that this is so fucked that I don't want nice things any longer.

And I look at the way I've survived almost every attempt what wants us gone has made to destroy me, and I realize it's precisely because I see differently that it wants me gone. It's why it wants difference destroyed, why it wants us all the same, all mindless, obedient, 'normal' people, easily controlled, easily done away with.

All the freaks I've known, all the fantastic queers, all the mad poets, all feral mystics and the incredible activists and truth-tellers and revolutionaries and meaning-makers all know what wants us gone.

And also know what needs us here.

What They Do Not Tell You

They do not tell you the Dead will ride you so far
You will almost join them, you
half-alive, standing between meaning
and meaning, the stuff you purchase
and the stuff that matters.

They do not tell you, but then you know
the dead who ride you matter, and so
you listen, here, in sleep and waking
and on-coming cars that aren't your death and
warriors and villains and blood-soaked earth.

Her death, and your life, flowing out
where later weeds take hold, and flowers
remembering what others forget, remembering
what others could not hear, there,
between stone and stone and earth.

The City at the Gates of The Dead

They do not tell you you shall die their deaths
Nor what you will become, still living
half sleeping, half waking, blooded
vessel flowing over from rim,
to stone
to now.

Brigid In The Dumpster, Brân In The Bad Heroin

He's fumbling with a flashlight. I'm drunk tonight, stumbling home. I shouldn't stop. I stop.

He's fumbling with the batteries, his movements erratic. One into the slot with the spring ("these fucking springs," he says) and then another but it slips and flies and it's on the ground next to me.

I'm sitting on the ground next to him. He's beautiful, really. Hairy, muscular, his face the sort one would wish to smile upon each morning.

He smells of piss and shit.

"You heard of dialysis?" he asks.

I nod, I light a cigarette, I give him one.

"I'll need it when I'm 40," he says. "The heroin does that. I can't piss." And then he's crawling on the ground looking for a battery.

"How old are you?" I ask, trying to light his cigarette again.

"35," he says, dropping his cigarette, twitching. "I use everyday, but this shit's bad, man."

It is. He shouldn't be twitching on heroin like this.

He shouldn't have the energy of thirty suns and the focus of a child if it were what he thought he was shooting.

"I think they cut it. If I pass out" (and here the batteries fly across the concrete),"– I don't know, man."

I went looking for something tonight, or someone.

Brân, actually. Pulled 40 feathers out from a squirrel-gnawed stag vertebrae found near the Pagan Wall of Mont St. Odile. Hid the feathers from my host's cats, unwrapped the crow's foot found at the foot of a Buddha.

Everything smelled of death, of carrion, everything smelled of Brân, and I'm on the pavement near a busy intersection, sitting cross-legged, gathering batteries.

"It's not like this usually," he says. His name is Mike. I gave him my name first. We'd met before, he was certain.

He was right, I suspected.

"I usually just crawl into bed when I shoot up."

For the first time tonight, I'm relieved. He's got a bed, somewhere safe, somewhere besides this asphalt.

"Where's home?" I ask. "I can help you get there."

Mike took awhile to answer. He'd spent the last 20 minutes trying to put batteries into a flashlight, a stolen LED wand. Four AAA batteries, tiny, miniscule in his muscular but swollen hands.

I didn't press. I picked up the batteries again, handing them back to him one at a time.

"It's just receipts, man! It's great. Clean. I just gotta get outta there by 7 in the morning. I even wrote 'em a thank-you card."

Years of social work and decades of reading taught me to wait for the unraveling of a story. You don't push or prod or pull. The words come in their time. We are our own best narrators, even when jacked-up on bad heroin.

Mike and I jolted together at a sudden noise. A taxi pulled up feet away, a man stepped out. Bold, clean, well-dressed, young. Probably another Amazon worker, or maybe Google. All privilege and wealth and bliss. Never a bad heroin trip.

The man sneered at us, likely 15 years our junior. He was staring at a heroin-addict fumbling with a flashlight smelling of piss, and a punk sitting next to him on the pavement, smoking a cigarette. We were trash on the street, nothing more. Loathing and disgust lined his face as he turned from us.

Mike fumbled with the batteries some more. I'd offered a few times, and he refused. His hands were the size of my face, he couldn't bend his fingers. Fluid retention, bad liver probably, bad kidneys definitely.

"You remember when you could just put batteries in?" he asked. We were friends, it seemed. Or comrades. I'm honored by this, though I've had it easier than him.

"Yeah–" I start to answer, but the batteries fall out again, his oafish fingers failing to grip. "Mike?" I asked, slightly impatient. "Can I help?"

He finally handed the thing to me. He stood up, adjusting his jacket several times. I slipped the third and fourth battery into the slots, replaced the cover, and turned it on.

Bright light-emitting diodes near-blinded me. I handed it back to him, fingering the gnawed bone in my pocket.

"The dumpster's soft with all the receipts," he replied, finally returning to our earlier conversation. "I need this to see in there."

I looked to where he pointed, a blue recycling dumpster. "You sleep there?"

"Yeah," he nodded, his spasms starting to slow. "Fucking bad heroin. I think there's meth in it or something."

As if on cue, an emergency vehicle drove by, run by the county. "Sobering Van," we call them. It stopped, turned on its lights, and the guy in the passenger seat stepped out, his hands already gloved.

"Hey, Mike?" he asked, walking towards us. "You okay?"

Mike backed away, visibly composing himself, patting down his clothes and squaring his shoulders. "I'm fine. They're gonna put a catheter in me, I'm not going. You ever had one of those stuck up your cock?"

The responder signed, shaking his head. "Just checking you're okay," and then he looked at me.

I told him what I could, what I'd gathered. I identified myself as a social worker, told the man about the bad heroin.

"Yeah," he nodded. "That's not just heroin there."

We both looked at Mike together, the terrified, beautiful man shaking involuntarily, his arms flailing.

"I'll check up on him in an hour," he told me, returning to the van. He thanked me, though I'd done nothing.

Nothing at all.

I looked at Mike. I looked at the dumpster. I reached into my pocket, pulled out the gnawed bone which has held feathers for Brân on my altar this last year. Bone from a dead deer on a temple mountain in Álsace, feathers from crows from everywhere, and a man, shaking, destroyed in this modern city, sleeping in a dumpster.

The City at the Gates of The Dead

   I stared. I'd gone looking for my gods tonight, somewhere out on the streets, away from their altar.
   And there was Brighid, there in that dumpster, the man's hearth. And here was Brân, here in that bad heroin, Mike's confrontation with death, here with one of his bards despairing at his mediocre efforts. Some gods are small enough to care about the heroin-addict in the dumpster. I hope I am always small enough to care, too.

Maybe,
Another Vein

(an Equinox meditation at the End of the World)

Maybe another vein. Some new device will come out, something which, for hours on end, will dull the bodily rage we feel after a third-of-day's labor.

We'll come home tired, driving across hot asphalt past ghosts of forests, over corpse of bison, elk, and "Indian," after hours of coding, or answering phones. Level-voiced women and men will soothe us with promises of a bright weekend, great beach weather, they'll advise, between cloying advertisements for Christmas sales and New Year's parties.

Interspersed, the assurances—the President said this, Congress will do that. Arguments between themselves, left-hand right-hand both stroking the slicked-up phallus before glowing altars with new operating systems and lifted faces.

We'll grumble to each other—she's not doing what she promised, he's violating the Constitution, never once daring to plumb the depths of mythic paper and civic religion because it's Friday.

Prices rise for salad greens we don't eat anyway, for apartments in neighborhoods we wouldn't bother to live in. Gas goes down and we have a little extra money, gas goes up and maybe we'll take a bus.

Sorting bits of paper into green bins and bottles into blue, we'll smile, having done enough.

Black man dead. Another Black man dead. Black kid dead. Muslim arrested, more Muslims arrested, a Black man shot a woman, a Black crowd burned a mom-and-pop shop.

New iPhone, though, and 2 more miles per gallon, and anyway the kids gotta go to practice, the mortgage's gotta be paid.

Maybe we'll find another vein. The floods, the droughts, the landslides, the blizzards, the weather is always something, isn't it? New lightbulb to poison the ocean, don't eat that fish if you're pregnant, retirement might not be there, we might not be either.

We'll cling. We'll claw, grasp, choke and grab and clutch and cling to things supposed to be. This is America, you know, this could be better but we'll get there and how come they want to kill us?

Spirits scream from dying forests, but they'll build some low-income housing to make up for it. Rivers dead, but desalination plants will make it better.

Can't get in that vein anymore, but there are others. Between the toes so no one knows, like the time we didn't sort paper from plastic in that bin. Heated and injected into the thigh, if you really need the eye–you can always make due.

We'll argue. Divine from the cards, from the stars, from the history book and the talk-shows, pundits and putrefaction but anyway, I've gotta go to work and how many jobs will that really make anyway?

Water shut-off in cities full of Black folk so we don't care. Water wars in Ireland but that's so far away, water pumped from before the days of walking apes but we gotta grow our food, can't just go without.

Maybe, just maybe, there's another vein.

Choked streams, dead gods, mountains tumbled-down 'cause we can't live like the poor. Solar will save us, we'll shout, desert priests staring into the sun. Split some atoms, it's worth some tumors, and here's another famine but they're darker than us again.

Coders still flushed with money arguing about public transit from their plastic condos, staring at screens like the grease-covered fingers of the immigrant behind the counter. They'll never be the same, they merit more because they use their brain and we're all thumbing the same phones.

Barista and cook drunk-to-sleep, driver and builder slumped in soft chairs, kicking empty cans they're too tired to recycle and anyway we know it's too late.

Spirits screaming as they leave, gods silent as they withdraw, crops wilting in the fields, but man, maybe—there's another vein.

Flickering fantasies of zombies because we can't see the living-dead we churn out, the starving on our streets and raging behind the fences. Mindless things, no sense, no hope, no reason could possibly birth such terror.

Slurp a coffee picked by their hands, throw on a shirt sewn by their fingers, scroll for a pick-up on phones they'll never afford though they make them for you. Cheer on the soldiers returning from their slaughter, grumble 'bout the taxes ensuring their submission, change the channel when you can't watch their anger.

There's gotta be another vein, asses wiped on flesh of forest, muscles toned in gyms like factories, doggy day-cares and organic juices and anyway you can't always care. Center, ground, breathe out that anxiousness, unsettled scores and open yourself to Spirit on your way to the co-op and eat a little less. Ethical flesh now and maybe more kale, corpse-cock and face-lifts The Science will find a way.

Postpone death, put it off, prop them up. Put on a new cock, pull up the sags, smooth the skin and replace the bone. De-salt the sea, un-tar the sands. Here's a hybrid, half-petrol half-coal; here's a chimera, part-algae part-corn. Dam up the dying rivers, shore up the flooding seas. Move money there, borrow credit there, shine LEDs against the shadow of death's looming debt. Find another well for water, another vein of coal.

Maybe we'll find another vein.

Maybe there's another vein.

Maybe, another.

Maybe.

The City At The Gates
Of The Dead

I.

I was looking for my cat, but I met him instead,
there on that blasted hill in the Otherworld.

I wake into the city, the city which stretches from borough to borough, neighborhood to neighborhood, downtown to downtown across the earth.

I wake into a city that does not know my gods, the Singers in the Dark. I am a foreigner, though I'm "from here." I worship "foreign" gods, though they live everywhere, sing from every part of the dark.

I wake and tread through streets soaked with rain; rain which washes from the sky the haze of car exhaust, the particulate of industry. Like gods, like the dead, I walk as if invisible, unknown, and unheard.

As long as we've been human, we've clustered together along sea-shores or river-banks, along lakes or in fertile valleys. We've done this for millennia, though they seem new. Paris–founded by a Celtic tribe more than 2000 years ago; London a little younger or a little older, depending how you parse it. These seem old, yet are far from the oldest in Europe and are young, infants compared to the ancients of the East.

And there are the much younger ones. The city into which I wake each morning is but a century-and-a-half old, founded by slaughterers eager to rape the hills of ancient Cedar, Spruce and Pine, selling tree-corpses down-coast to build the sprawling cities of California. And around this city has sprung more cities, cities called towns, cities called sub-urbs, webs of streets connecting them in the great modern nightmare called Metropolis.

The city has always been a thing we've done. We've always huddled to-gether, gathering ourselves near others. In all the history of the world, the individual, the loner, the fully independent solitary has been a fantasy. Even ascetics and hermits relied on others, teaching their wisdom in exchange for food. We've gathered together in villages, settling in a place for awhile or, if it were a very good place, forever. We need others, as much as pretend we don't. We need the land beneath us, as much as we ignore it and destroy it.

II.

He wore a black hooded tunic, his face familiar and ancient.
I knew whom he was from, but I didn't know him.
'Watch the city with me,' he beckoned, and showed me a village.

Another train derailed today. Or was it yesterday? I can't be sure.

Carrying oil from the earth on iron rails which helped build the city I live in, carrying that oil to be refined so it could be burned so we, gathered in all the many cities, the urban and rural and in-between, can have more things.

The train derailed. "Kaboom," it said, and our cars say "vroom, vroom," and at most we shake our heads and head to work, head to shop, head home in our "vroom vroom" cars as another train goes Kaboom.

It goes Kaboom like the bombs we drop on people in the deserts to get their oil.

It goes Kaboom like the explosions of pipelines along rivers, like the si-lent Kabooms we don't hear and don't see, the massive leaks into ancient rivers and forever-damaged lands, the Kaboom of a village starving or a town flooding or a glacier melting.

This whole thing's a mess, and the city is everywhere. All the world's a city now, except where it isn't. The photos from space show dark and very bright, illumination into the stellar abyss fired not by internal fusion of stars but the burning of coal ripped from mountains. To power the city we once dug below the mountain; to power the world-city we rip off its top.

Do not mistake me--the rural is no innocent place, no idyllic escape from the death of the city.

I first woke to the world in Appalachia, along the eastern stretch of valley beginning the foothills of those mountains. On the bus to school I'd stare out the window upon mountaintops sheared of forest for the paper mill. On the hills further east were the explosions and the blackened streams to get at the coal beneath those sheared forests.

To the south was the alternative, the nuclear power plant where my uncle and my papaw worked as contractors. My mamaw got a settlement from the owners for each of their deaths, their skulls swollen to bursting with massive tumors. My father took care of his brother in his last days. To this day, I'm harrowed like the earth by his tales, his stories of hosing down his feces-covered twin—they could not afford hospice for him as he died.

Near the city into which I wake, it is the same.

Travel west over water to a peninsula, where there resides the last re-maining rainforest in the United States, the breathing ancient pillars of the Hoh. Haunting miles of those silent giants intermittently broken by clear-ings and sprawling homes with hand-painted signs demanding the urban governments allow them to cut more trees.

On a warm summer day, by that ancient forest, sunlight and joy soaking my skin, I stumbled through a parking lot of a gas-station, blinking back the light as I read the bumper stickers on trucks. Their slogans stopping my heart: "Clearcut America," proclaimed one, and another, "One less pesky forest."

And to live in the American rural, one must have a car.

To have a car, one must destroy the world.

Kaboom went that train, yesterday or maybe the day before–I can't be sure. And which train? There are so many. Last year was the record for 'unintentional releases' on trains: 114, or one every 76 hours. At this rate, why bother counting them all?

Besides, we need that oil for our world-city.

III.

In that faded non-light, light from the earth or from the soul,
I stood with him and watched the village.
People gathered, lived, ate, fucked, sang, farmed, wove, and carted.
And Kaboom, and then suddenly they all died.

The city is the urban and the city is the rural. Those living far from the seas of concrete we call cities require the urban to survive. Mounted to walls in those idyllic homes are the flat-screens translating the digital into images, and they, like the Lady of Shalott, are as free as she, bound to their seclusion, forbidden ever to see the real beyond the image.

But the images are no more real than the fantasy of the Modern. We're surrounded, drowning, in Baudrillard's hyperreal, gazing placidly at pastoral scenes or clicking furiously to kill orcs in flat forests. We raze the forests and then pixellate them, flocking to theaters to see sweeping depictions of them, looking at life elsewhere.

If we've some fortune, there's some forest in our city. The city into which I wake has forest. Some are outposts of the ancients in ignored places, some tracks through trees upon which scores of joggers publicly exorcise the demons of their workday. There's little quiet in those places as they pass, but there's so little forest in any city, even in such a forested city, that we have to take what we get.

And all the world's owned now, except where it's been stolen back. I stole back some forest park nearby for awhile, forlorn, abandoned, un-tended. The only attention it ever got was that of a few building contractors, looking for cheap places to dump their trash: old bathroom furnishings, toilet seats, appliances removed and sent tumbled-down into a stream-bed to make more modern someone's home. Looking into that ravine filled with trash I saw again the viridian hills of Appalachia, the silent grottoes and hidden caves filled with old cars, refrigerators, washing machines, corpses of machines built to make the life of a modern worker easier. Rusted metal and enamel near where I wanted to play, a boy of 8, napping one afternoon upon a burial mound on "private property."

I do not think that mound is still there. In many places, you can level a burial mound just as you can level a mountain, even more so if you're doing it for profit and claim it'll "create jobs." Because everyone wants to work, because everyone needs to work, because all the world is owned, and all the peoples within it. You're worth something, because you work for someone, you turn the machines, create the codes, hand over the sandwich and count the change. If you do not work, you are not yet owned, and to be your own person, to be un-owned, is to be hungry, invisible, homeless...foreign. To refuse to submit is to be criminal. To refuse to be owned is rebellion. To refuse to consent is deemed at best eccentric, but most often insane.

IV.

Not all of them died, though.
As I watched with him, survivors gathered in the ruins, rebuilding, a stronger and
more vibrant settlement than before.
More people, more buildings, stronger walls, more singing.
And then another destruction.

The city into which I wake, the city into which I nightly sleep, is a city full of unheard gods, the Singers in the Darkness.

Streetlamps fill the night with pale light, recently changed to rotting-flesh sallow LED to save money, not the earth. To save the earth (kaboom goes the oil-train) we'd stop driving, stop working for others, stop buying things we don't need or even really want.

We'd even turn the lights off.

The lights block out those older lights, those farther lights from distant black shores, great illuminations in the abyssal darkness into which we once stared—which still stares back. Bathing concrete and asphalt in ghostly light, washing sombre faces and tree branch and flower-bed of the colors of life, the lights shine not into the Darkness, only into our distracted sleep.

They make safe the streets from criminals, I've heard, though it seems easier to commit a crime when you can see than when you are blind. The lights, I think, protect from someone else, the Singers in the Darkness, waiting, whispering, chanting beyond the city from the worlds between and beyond the walls.

There's no place for gods in a city where there's no place for poets or the poor, no place for the dead in a city that fears shadows, no place for spirits in a world that cannot abide not-seeing.

But in a city with no place for poets, the poets persist.

In a city with no place for gods, the Singers wait, unquiet, staring from the Darkness.

The city in which I awake, the city in which I sleep, the city in which I write is the whole human world, a gate to the Human, a walled-enclave from the divine. The whole world is made up of walls, fences to keep humans in; fences to keep humans out; prisons and cubicles and schools and cages where we gather and are gathered. The homeless fill the beds of shelters; the poor crowd the jails; the workers and their autos (kaboom) clog the streets to and from the places we are demanded, the places we are shunted, and the places we are allowed.

A Kindness of Ravens

In the downtowns, towers huddle together like the rain-drenched workers below them, waiting to cross streets to get to buses or cars, to get to home or lunch or another place to shop. The homeless beg on corners and in doorways, and it is the same in São Paolo as it is San Francisco, the same in Paris as it is in Orlando. The poor in the shanty and the poor in the city share blood of a different kindred, bearing upon their faces the stolen birthrights of the gods we've forsaken and the forests we've slaughtered.

The Singers in the Darkness have not stopped singing.

They come through the gates to greet us, they flee through the gates at our approach.

We are so loud—our cars, music, jackhammers, fights and laughter, our stereos which surround, our engines which rumble past what needs silence to sing. We shout at nothing, a screen across which men run across false-grass. We thumb and touch and stare at the smaller screens, white tendrils clinging close to the tympani of our skull.

In these images, these frames, there can be nothing else but what we are shown. Not gates but tableaux, processions of shadows from which we weave meaning. She? She was shot. See? This kitten has had a bad day.

"What are you looking at?" We say to the mad, or the child, or pet, or the poet. "Everything else," they could say, but we can't hear them.

V.

I watched as he stood silent as ages past.
Another settlement, this time a town, next time a city, next time another.
Each time some calamity destroyed them, each time they rebuilt.
I'd been looking for my cat, not for the history of humanity, but when you ask the gods for something, you take what they give you, you witness what they show you.
And finally, a last city, grand, beautiful, the strongest of all,
encompassing the world. The strength and brilliance and art of humanity woven into those walls and towers, a city that would not, could not end.

And I saw what was coming.

All the world's walled now, except for the worlds between the walls, the Singers in the Darkness. We dwell between wall and wall, prison and home, school and work, city and city, all connected by roads and rails.

Kaboom says the oil train, says the dynamite in the mountaintop, says the tumor in the nuclear-workers' brain, says the gun of the policeman, says the missile of the drone, says the dying of the earth.

What we've wrought is glory, is it not? I type and you read my words, I dial and you hear my voice. Strawberries in winter, transatlantic flights now with wi-fi. Medicines to undo aging, to harden the phallus past 70, to impregnate the womb past 50. Cars (vroom vroom) to whisk us to work, or to mountains (kaboom), pocket-toys to help us find sex or restaurants, lights to shine at the darkness, bombs to destroy cities.

What we've wrought cannot last forever, and is dying.

The Singers in the Darkness scare me with their songs, they terrify me with their tales.

They are singing our death song, they are keening our end.

An oil train derailed yesterday. Or was it tomorrow?

It won't matter much longer.

I watched the explosions, the annihilation.
The disintegrated walls, the immolated children, the flattened cities.
I watched with him, who serves whom I serve, and we were silent.
I waited for stirring in the ruins, for awakening in the rubble,
but I knew nothing would come.
No city could spring again from those ruins.
I turned away and met his face, sombre, beautiful as death but not dead,
a bard of the Singers in the Darkness.
"You understand now?" He asked.
I said I did. I don't think I did, not really.
I understood what I saw, but I'll never understand why.

"Good," he said, nodding, and turned, opening to me the Gates of the Dead.

After The Fire, Invisible

I wanted a fuck, a fire, a cup of tea
Or maybe that's what you wanted, maybe
not the fuck, or maybe, but I thought you said
"I'm cold," and thought I'd bring you warmth.

And this burnt flesh's not yours—right?
I'd like to think I'd know it from
this charred wood, this ash, this melted plastic
these still-hot beams. I'll be here awhile

sifting through these ruins, this toppled stone,
under warped metal, looking for something
that might remain—some fucking bit of hair,
some flesh, some bone. Anything.

But you helped me set this, you smiled
as we told old stories, bound too close
around our frigid hearts. You smiled, I thought,
when I said, 'I'd seen that too.'

The City at the Gates of The Dead

And really. I think I remember, or maybe wrong,
that moment before we lit this, from gathered
bits of paper, tinder and words pyred, torched,
to burn this whole shit down.

The idea was mine, maybe, the words most
also mine, so many, because I'd hoarded them
longer than you might think, but you
brought some of your own, too.

I'll confess, I guess, if you're really gone. I'll say
that maybe I'd dragged you in, you'd only wanted a light
a bit or warmth, something to see by, something quiet
or something tame. Not this blackened mess.

I'm sorry, not for this, but that I'm still not sure
if you made it out. Did I torch you to warm myself
Or you? I'll never know. I can't be to blame, I saw
something there you couldn't see.

You, standing near me, too close for you, maybe
not close enough for me, cowering in shadowed
corners, hidden in your quiet, unheard.
How could I not burn this down? But still–

I don't know if you made it. I can't find you
in this rubble, but I doubt you really died.
You're too good at hiding, being the one thing
you really wish you would never be.

Perhaps you watch unseen, maybe waiting
for me to leave, and I will, when I'm done.
But I'm leaving things for you, before I go.
In case you made it out, and still need some warmth

or another stupid poem we should have burned
before I torched your world. And I've nothing
else to say, 'cept if you gotta hide,
just know I'm out alive, burning and unhurt.
And am hoping you are, too.

She Sends A Flood Upon The World

There's a violence in love. Not the domestic sort, the horror of a lover hitting the beloved; nor the self-immolation of the scorned. Rather, the mystery of the "Winged Serpent," called by some the Peacock Angel.

When fear and desire become each other, Divine Twins fighting and fucking, brightness and darkness in shimmering, relentless beauty, wielding a sword called Love.

A fire rises between them, called Compassion by some, Violence by others, the flame of Creation, the pyres of Destruction.

There are two peacocks, the one shining, radiant, sun in a blue sky reflected upon the surface of water; the other, crimson, hot blood unseen in the caverns our our flesh. One is the festival in midsummer, the other the winter revolt.

Both are called Love.

It was Che Guevera who said, "At the risk of seeming ridiculous, let me say that the true revolutionary is guided by a great feeling of love. It is impossible to think of a genuine revolutionary lacking this quality."

A seer sought my soul and saw there this: Me, kneeling in ash, covered in ash, before a brazier filled with ash, a blade in my hand.

A shaman led me to a hill over Llyn Dinas to meet a dragon. "I will teach you to breathe fire," it had said, before the giant took me.

And so here I am, Bard of the Raven King who destroyed an island, child of a Sea-Witch who floods the world, initiate of some strange revolutionary order whose power comes not from weapons and armaments but from forests and the unseen.

I am trying to re-awaken the land against a coming slaughter while toppling would-be tyrants from their fragile thrones.

I'll not know if I ever succeed until I see that Bard again, there on that hill.

But that's never just been up to me.

44

Love Notes From
The Abyss, II

"I am half-sick of shadows," she said, and so are you.

Here's her tower, here's his fortress, and before them both parade the world—like for you, there in the world of light, walled from the Abyss. She stares, and he, at all the world before them. The bloody cup, the two lovers, neither fear nor joy. He on his throne, her at the loom, the mirror, the window.

Outside the fertile land, ungrasped.
Outside the desolation, unbroken.
Life parades before them, but they cannot live it.
Magic is displayed before them, but they cannot hold it.

To both the Lady of Shalott and to the Fisher King, a knight appears, and this is what the poets had tried to tell you:

The unasked question isn't for you to pose. but for you to answer.

And only another can ask it.

Perceval

Do not be pressed into fear
By the pushing of spears.
–Lorna Smithers, The Bull of Conflict

I.

"People cannot rule themselves. They need someone to tell them what to do. They're too stupid."

Crimson and night the colors about me as I speak to the king. I can see his staff, his scepter a bit too heavy, tilted in his hand, weighted like a mace, weighted like his words.

I cannot believe the words I'm hearing. They do not fit the demeanor of the regent, the lauded generosity, even his self-stated Anarchism. I want to challenge him, but I'm losing my nerve, my arm tired from the blows, my mind spinning, my eyes darting about for an ally.

But I'm here alone, sitting before a vision of seductive human power while he details a glorious vision of the future, and we're at war.

It's funny, you know. I'm no warrior. I'm not even all that serious, even when a cop is bashing my head against the hood of a police car. I make jokes, I jeer and act ridiculous because the world's all too serious. I prefer tea over whiskey, like I'm an old British woman with her doilies.

I'm no warrior, though I'm sitting amongst them, people I admire, respect, perhaps even crush upon. I walked in with a priestess of battle talking of warrior dead and Alder shields; I, myself, am devoted to a warrior-king-god and the raging giants of land who hold his flesh, but I'm only a bard. A bard who'd fight to the death to end Capitalism, sure, but I'd rather weave its end with my words, not the other sort of sword.

I'm here, guest of warriors, wilting under the dazzling vision of an intoxicating future, wishing I'd more tea in my cup or that another would extricate me from this battle. Not quite cowardice–I could have fled a bit ago, cited discomfort or some false errand. I'd been fighting the urge to say "you scare me," despite how frightful I found the tilting king.

II.

He's berating me, suddenly, and very well, almost with my own voice. "Why didn't you bother to educate yourself?"

Why'd he ask me if I had a Master's degree or just a Bachelor's? Why did I answer? I'm usually much better with these conversations, but I'm off-balanced, tripping over my own words. I parried, I tried to explain what my time in social work had taught me about non-profits, re-hashing the argument I'd proffered before.

"So you have a Masters in Social Work, or…?"

"Neither," I say. I didn't finish college, an odd wound suddenly re-opened. And suddenly I have nothing to say, all my words invalidated, just as he notes my age and sagely advises me I'm not old enough to understand. I try to explain how I've educated myself, how I'd read every book on economics, and politics, Lacanian psychoanalysis and Critical Theory, Zizek and Baudriallard —

"But you're not educated. You never bothered, why?"

This was going poorly. My eyes dart around the room, trying to find solace, to ignore the insult. Suddenly I'm telling him about my poverty, and the Christian college I had to leave, strangely offering up my soul.

"How old are you?" He asks, and again I confess my faults.

"Ah," he says, pouncing. "You're at an earlier cycle; you can't see the truth I see. When you reach my age, you see what needs to be done."

Why's an anarchist bard wilting at such talk? I weave meaning, but I am here de-meaned, belittled, berated, an adolescent before an Adult, an Authority, one who knows, one who knows that he knows.

I keep looking around to see if others are noting this conversation, the artfully-woven insults, my awkward poise, wishing for interruption. But I know better: I need to endure this, I need to hear these words myself. And it was I who'd challenged him in the first place; not personally, of course, as I knew him only as a Name, branded-large like others but without the cult status. He's not quite a celebrity occultist, not the head of a gay-witch triad with product lines or 30 books to his name. Head of a mage-order, sure, and his magic screams through every artful word, but even that order's not the Empire he's thirsting to build.

This man's brilliant, you can tell. Likable, too, charming without being cloying. And he's actually trying to build something, something most don't ever bother to do. And not just build something, but build something useful, something everyone could benefit from, not just those who can buy-in, pay for the retreats or the seminars, take the five-year courses and attend the parties. So why the fuck are we fighting?

III.

I came to this Pagan thing late, I guess, though I've been a "cultural" Pagan for most of my adulthood. I had all these ideas about what it meant, what others probably did and believed, what sorts of rituals go on when most aren't looking, and particularly, what sorts of stances most Pagans held about the world around them.

It's enlightening to hear the surprise of others when I try to explain what I'm on about, what sorts of things I say make others angry. I usually smile and sigh when they say, 'but I thought you were all anti-capitalists?' or 'wait–there are racist Pagans? How?'

It's the same surprise we all have at some point. I spoke to a new friend about this under a tree outside a conference at which I spoke—his own friends were surprised to hear we're not all vegetarians. Another friend heard for the first time that some of us believe all the gods are part of one god. That same weekend, I watched hundreds of people laugh flippantly before entering a ritual for The Morrígan; from their shocked, somber exit afterward, I suspect many suddenly discovered that gods actually exist.

But anyone can call themselves a Pagan, just as any can call themselves a Queer or an Anarchist. I wield all three, though I know they're just words, meaningful in some contexts, enraging in others, meaningless otherwise.

Wiccans understandably rage that the traditions and lineages they've nurtured now can mean anything one likes. I can declare myself a Wiccan High Priest after reading a book. I can claim to be a Shaman and charge money to teach enlightenment in corporate training seminars without ever having seen the spirit world. To back up my story I could list years of training, anonymous teachers and secret lineages and, with enough magic (usually just an advertizing budget) and enough followers, I can become invincible, a king amongst earnest peasants.

Pagan is a word so large to encompass the world if it so chose. There've been efforts (rightly fought) to describe indigenous religions as Pagan, to re-inscribe Hindu and African-Animist beliefs as the same thing that's being done in the West. It's a beautiful idea, a grand vision, but frightful and wrong because of who's doing the naming. Whites, mostly men, with some western education and the benefits of modern security and ease may correctly identify correlations and similarities, but like Crowley and Gardner, their own colonialism is invisible.

It's not we who get to name what they do. To identify with the oppressed, we must become the oppressed and relinquish what makes us oppressive. I'm a gay white man living in a highly-developed American city; I do not know the oppression of a woman on the floor of a textile mill in Cambodia after sacred spirits her people worshiped were uprooted. Not only do I not know her oppression, I sustain it with my need for clothes and my failure thus far to destroy the system which profits her owner.

Pagans seem natural allies with such folks; we want the forests, we want the traditions, we want the breathing ancestors and the singing spirits, the gods and ancients weaving throughout our lives and communities. I'd thought that was what Paganism meant, long before I met other Pagans. I hadn't yet seen the rows of books published from re-formulated indigenous knowledge; I hadn't yet read the screeds against the invasion of social justice into Wicca or the accusations that my writing "colonizes Paganism with anti-Capitalism." I didn't yet know that Pagan can mean whatever one wants it to mean.

IV.

How much have the elders sold us out, genuflecting to the academy, the establishment, the tabloid press. In return for this bargain we have gained precisely nothing. The supposed freedoms we have been granted are empty. Late capitalist culture simply does not care what our fantasy dress up life is like as long as we work our zero hour contracts, carry our mobile phones and keep consuming.
—Peter Grey, Rewilding Witchcraft

I'm wilting under the assault of his words, this brilliant man chastising me for my failure to learn, my churlish attempts to critique his grand vision.

"You've read Peter Grey's *Rewilding Witchcraft*, yeah?" I ask, hoping for a shared reference.

He laughed, muttered something about nonsense. "No–why don't you summarize it for me?"

And suddenly I'm trying to form words quickly, like a bad student scribbling a book review an hour before class. "Uh–" I said, feeling the fool. "Look–the point's about…about how Pagan elders have–wait, no. He's writing about how we've sold out, decided it's better to have pentacles on headstones then an end to imperialist wars, to have our nice things instead of a surviving planet, how we've dulled–"

"Not everyone wants the wars," he said, and I agreed, and eased, but then I lost the thread.

"In 25 years, only Corporations will have any power or say. They're golems, indestructible…"

I'd read his essay on this. "I liked that article!" I interrupted, because I did, and I'd rather be friends. But I'd also thought he'd missed the point, but it was a great start.

"It's true. This is all about power, which is why everything about privilege and other nonsense you hear in social justice circles is wrong."

I was about to choke on his words even as I watched the mortified eyes of a woman glare at whatever fragments she'd just caught. Her face was unreadable, but I could not imagine she was pleased.

There's almost a point there, which is most frightening. Privilege describes a power-relation, but I've seen it abused to mean whatever one wants. I've heard folks speak of "disabled privilege" and "minority privilege" with straight faces and no irony. I've read a lot of New-Right writers; I fear their influence upon intellectuals in Paganism more than that of the Archetypalists. They, more than anyone, threaten to re-form our beliefs into outright, powerful, and true hatred, and they say the exact same thing–it is power which matters.

He's right, and they're right, but they're both quite wrong, but that was hardly the place to explain this and besides–I'm elsewhere.

Water's lapping at my feet in the mist, clear snow melted with rain soaking my boots. He's talking elsewhere, haranguing my foolishness amongst the black and red tapestries as I listen from a lake edge.

It's raining, but I'm not wet, and there are giants amongst me, and I am taller, made of stone, forged from rocks and streams. I am not here, and I am also here, and I'm thinking of Alder, of fallen kings and undefeated mountains.

"We need power, and for that we need money. And then we'll found institutions, a legislative body, a–"

"That's terrifying," I all but shout. A legislative body? To make rules for Pagans?

And yet fuck is this vision intoxicating, almost as strong as the place my soul re-visited.

V.

I could almost advocate for his vision of a future better than he can.

A Pagan leader was arrested for possession of child pornography; after his arrest, the internet flooded with accounts of people who'd endure abuse by him, and one was left to wonder why no-one had acted before. With a grand Pagan council, perhaps he would have been stopped earlier.

Multiple witches have been shown to have plagiarized other sources, selling spiritual knowledge as completely their own. If you count up the number of years certain Brand-Named Pagans claim to have studied under mysterious teachers, you find a lot of people who apparently initiated at 6 years of age And speaking of early initiations, there are still those who advocate sexual initiation of underage children. A television warlock outed several critics as witches and publicly wished one victim to think about him while she's raped, and yet he hosts large festivals and gets no censure from those invited to reap profit with him. With a certification body and a reporting structure, we could force people to speak the truth about themselves and chasten those who advocate abuse of children or the vulnerable in the name of profit.

Fuck. With a legislative body, we could make rules on who gets to call themselves a Pagan! No more Atheo-Pagans or Christo-Pagans or Naturalist-Polytheists. We could have rules people have to obey about claiming Wiccan identification, or Feri/Faery, or perhaps an entire testing apparatus to verify someone who claims to be married to Loki or to have a direct line to Dionysos isn't just writing masturbatory fan-fic. No more racialist Heathens or fluffy-bunny woo-witches; no more Otherkin or Otherfaith or Other-anything except what we name as true and accepted.

It's almost glorious how much power we could wield thereafter. Imagine—with the coin we could have our own political parties, our own institutions, our own networks. More festivals, more conventions and conferences. More Pagan academics, perhaps our own media outlets, maybe our own political party and candidates. Blessed by our certainty of truth, we could fight the behemoth golems of Corporations, wage war on the polluters, support impoverished and oppressed communities like the Yezidis rather than urging military intervention.

We could have a brave new powerful Pagan future, and this would-be king's work would succeed where all our other efforts have failed.

But the waves of Llyn Dinas are lapping through my boots, and I felt like Galadriel giving Frodo back the ring.

VI.

For the master's tools will never dismantle the master's house. They may allow us to temporarily beat him at his own game, but they will never enable us to bring about genuine change.
-Audre Lorde

There's a way out of the horrors we've gotten ourselves into, but it will never be that easy. I bring this up when people ask me what we should do about Capitalism; I say this again about everything else. No one solution can work, nor should any of us hope to find a concise answer and easily-followed directions to restore the forests and the gods, to build safe and thriving communities of honor and love rather than hatred and privilege.

To any would-be king's answer, we should answer in return:

People must rule themselves; there's no other way. We cannot hope for benevolent dictators or kind benefactors to end our suffering and fractious-ness and abuse. No great ruler will make racism go away, no brilliant queen will re-grow the forests.

We beg the government to give us recognition, to restrain the police they hire to kill us, to protect our sexual preferences and drinking water and children from the very same abusers who bankroll their political campaigns. The answer isn't the coin, it's the fucking soul, the reclaiming of our sover-eignty not just as will-to-power but responsibility-to-love.

Paganism isn't a religion; it's a collection of religious stances of folks finding succor and joy in each other's presence, some recognition in the others who claim the word: a shared understanding. I worship gods, and some of those dwell in trees that are dying to make way for our cars. I revere the dead, and many more will die at the hands of police or soldiers or polluters before I join them. But an atheo- or Christo- or Neo- Pagan can see the same thing as a polytheist or a witch: choking oceans, bitter air, murdered Black folk and caged immigrants and starving children.

It's around such a center we cling. We need no Authority to lead us, only a myriad of sovereign souls favoring love over profit, truth over fame, and revolution over the security of a gated plantation.

VII.

If you meet the Buddha on the road, kill him.
–Linji

"I see things as they really are," he'd said to me, and it is here I feel pity, not anger.

"We should be careful, right? 'Cause everyone thinks they alone see the truth, you know?"

"They're wrong," he said. "But I actually do see things as they really are. I was trained to see this."

I don't know what to say of this. My out was coming, a friend had begun to notice my desperate attempts to disengage. I'd never been so uncomfortable before, even when being told I was being arrested or fired.

"Look," I finally said. "What you want to do terrifies me. It's the sort of thing I already fight elsewhere, the very thing which makes us lazy and easily controlled and keeps us from fighting Capitalism. I undermine that wherever I find it—I'd have to undermine that, too. I find you dangerous."

"Then we're of the same opinion about each other," he replied, and I guess we'd declared war.

I cannot help but think of another conversation. The day before I left for this convention, I'd been sitting at a coffee shop, overhearing two anarchists speak of how miserable the world is, how fucked we all are, and how the only way to survive would be to hide in tiny enclaves as the world crumbles.

They seemed too young to be so cynical. I interjected once or twice; our conversation was convivial, they invited me in. But something went wrong ten minutes in. The male of the couple, a ferocious, rage-filled and beautiful man, had suggested all whites are supremacists. I disagreed, I'd reminded him that there's always the "race traitor," the folks who side with the oppressed rather than claiming their privilege. "Some open the gates from the inside, undermining the power we're supposed to inherit."

He shook with anger. I watched his muscled chest tense, his beautiful eyes fill with hatred. "The only whites who can be trusted are those who know they should be shot, who know they're too dangerous to be around anyone else because they can't stop hurting people."

"I'm sorry–I've made you angry," I said, feeling rather miserable. The man had been delightful, fascinating, but I'd suddenly become his enemy. He stood up with his companion and left, pushing the copy of *A Pagan Anti-Capitalist Primer* I'd handed them as a gift back towards me. That conversation felt like a failure, though I know I could have done nothing to undo the harm others have done to him.

But there's one thing I'd wished I'd said, not to that anger but to that fear beneath it, the same thing I'd wished I'd said before I'd left the toppling king. Though both men were different, one 15 years younger and one 15 years older, I'd say the same thing:

You're too young to be ruled by fear.

And also too old to be ruled by fear.

The world's shit and getting worse, but without trust in each other, there's really no point fighting for anything. Any world we build, if it's not built for love, will be as miserable as what we've got now, because there's no love in Capitalism.

VIII.

How can you love the Other you have not seen, when you do not love the other that you have?

–Jesus, paraphrased

I fled that argument, practically crashing into friends who hid me in an elevator to have time to calm myself. I think I may have been fleeing my own rage, or maybe my own fear, but definitely my own love.

And from there I ran into another who'd heard in my shaking speech a panic and a feeling of unsafety. I spoke to her of what'd happened, how I'd felt trapped by the anger of another, and then I fled again, doubting everything I'd stood for, everything I'd come to say and hoped to help build. Why call myself a Pagan if it meant the seeking of power, why association with so many others if it meant so much strife?

"Hey," said a voice from someone I'd almost knocked over. "I have a gift for you."

It was a friend, one I'd not met before this weekend, but one who'd read my words many times and spoke kindly to them. I could barely look at her, my head swirling with doubt and torment as if ensorcelled.

"From Brigid's well, in Kildare," she said, handing me a small blue vial of water. "Keep doing what you're doing."

And another friend, soon after hugged me and said the same thing, and I could not help but laugh.

We're killing our gods to use these computers and to shop at our malls. We're slaughtering humans to keep commerce going and have nicer phones. We're imprisoning people and animals in cages to turn a profit, bombing villages and shattering mountains to drive our cars.

It's this which matters most. If what we do helps stop this, than we must do it. If what we do sustains this or supports this, then we must be stopped.

From the wells and springs and fires of Brighid comes this love, which is the opposite of fear. What we must build to fight what's coming cannot repeat the same errors as what we're fighting. What we wield to destroy the golems we've created cannot also destroy those whom the golems grind to dust, otherwise we become the same monsters we fight.

The stone in a foundation can support, or can be pried out to smash in a head. A wall around a city can defend, but can also imprison. A grand vision can just as easily liberate as it can maim. I worry for Pagans if this is all we can come up with, a society of order which could be used to protect the vulnerable or to shut them out completely, diminish and even silence voices we don't want to hear.

We must not fall to fear, no matter how sharp the spear-tips seem pushing on us. The multitude and the myriad may be raucous and disorganized, but so are forests and the wilds. They—not the structures and institutions of the society which destroys them—must be our teachers.

Awakening The Land

"Around the world, discontent can be heard. The extremists are grinding their knives and moving in as the machine's coughing and stuttering exposes the inadequacies of the political oligarchies and who claimed to have everything in hand. Old gods are rearing their heads, and old answers: revolution, war, ethnic strife."

--Paul Kingsnorth and Dougald Hine, The Dark Mountain Manifesto

To know a god, you must go mad.

We call it dis-enchantment, this sallow state of existence, the frayed-threads of the tapestry of meaning. Modernity we call it, and freedom, progress and arrival into a future without them.

Once Them. Once us. Them with us. We with Them.

Now—cut. Wounds cauterized in the searing heat of machined-mills, branches severed below the fork, roots encased in concrete, veins of memory collapsed.

We are disenchanted, disinherited, dis-tracted, led away, leaden feet sinking into grey dust of barren lands which cannot soak up the water falling from heavy, pregnant skies.

Scrambling up wet scree tumbling down upon iron rails, boots sodden, fingers pricked through upon needle of gorse, I climbed to ask them for help. One loomed far south of me, scraggly hair, unbearded, watching the man far below pretend comfort with heights. Behind and below, across the tracks and further in the snow-melt swollen river, the indifferent guardian waited, waited like water waits.

"Okay," I shouted, dizzied, guessing how long it'd take my companion to find my broken-necked corpse on the tracks. Would he find me before the train? Or likely find me after, even more mangled.

"Okay. I—uh. I'm actually—I can't climb anymore. Can we talk from here?"

Laughter, amusement, felt through the stone, shaking the rain.

"Ah...good. Sorry. I'm actually a really small person, and I don't think I can reach that rock and—yeah. So."

Attempts at formality would look more false than my bravado. They already know who I am, why I'm there. If the guardian in the river hadn't told them, the gate-hound would have, and even if they'd held their tongue, they're kin of him I'm there for. And I've no composure for pretense, a hundred-foot drop below my slipping grip.

"I was wondering if you'd help me?"

More laughter. Assent shouted through bone.

"Ah. Okay. Thanks!" It all suddenly seemed easy. Giants are good-natured, after all, even the child-slaying and beard-flaying ones. I almost let go the exposed tree-root which kept me from falling the hundred feet to the rails below, so relieved was I.

Their laughter continued. The Fool's often amusing, and I near laughed with them, noticing my predicament: *I couldn't get down.*

"Stride down like us," I heard, with voice clearer than through ears. "And give her our gift."

My boots are wet. I'm wet. Shirtless, covered in mud, hanging by roots and rocks. I am the water pouring down my skin, I'm soaking through myself into the rock and becoming the lake at the source of the river, and he's coming. They're there.

You don't have to go mad to see them, but you must abandon reason to keep them around after the sight. Giants, nymphs, ghosts—they're there, you've seen them maybe once but then looked away and forgot. Shaking off and away the vision, looking again, changing your view so they're not there on the second glance. Dis-enchanted.

We don't do this just with The Other, we do this with ourselves, particularly with desire. The Other is queer, sometimes we are, and like the man denying desire for another man in a world where only women are allowed, The Other is the queer we disallow. Easier to deny different desire when surrounded by others who also deny; easier to disallow god-giants when no-one else admits to them.

To dis-allow is to forbid; to dis-enchant is to de-ny, repudiate, withhold from ourselves what we thought occurred. Self-abnegation, sacrificial poverty of spirit so we can be what we're supposed to be, what is demanded of us. Resist the trembling lust for what your flesh desires and no thing queer enters into the world of self-controlled workers selling time for money.

"Money is extracted time," he shouted at me, and I shook. I shook like the time he pushed me back, wouldn't let me pass. I tried, he pushed again. I pushed back. Don't get in a pushing match with a giant.

I shook like the time he was in my head, rummaging there, sifting, sorting. "Who's this?" he said, one of the few times I've heard his voice with my ears.

"Just someone I desired," I answered, and he shook his head.

II.

We're drunk. I'm drunker, but he's pretty drunk too.

"Who's Brad?"

We're naked. We're usually naked when we sleep, and we're usually together when we sleep.

"Brad?" I'm drunk. I forgot who Brad is. There was Brett, a couple of Brians or at least one Brian and one Bryan.

"He must've been damn good."

I'm drunk and I don't know who he's talking about.

"I—I don't know a Brad." I'm pretty certain of this. I'm actually pretty certain I've never fucked a Brad.

He looks at me a bit askance, then smiles. "You moan his name when you sleep."

"Oh," I say, suddenly laughing, relieved. "You mean Brân?"

"Yeah, that's the name you're saying. Who's he?"

I moan a giant-god's name in my sleep. I guess this is weird. It's definitely queer, but no more than climbing a cliff-face in Snowdon to ask giants for help. Maybe slightly more queer than the giantess another saw straddling over me, wild, mountainous, rough. I was asleep when he saw this, in a tent amongst Alders on another land while a boar rummaged through my belongings; he was in Seattle, part-dreaming, I guess.

"He's mine, don't worry," she said to him. I wasn't there, or was—sorta. At least thirty birds had shat upon my tent and a few nearby in the morning, the only day that'd happened at that site. The Breton women camping nearby asked if I'd seen the *sanglier* who'd come from the mountain. I hadn't, nor had I seen the giantess, either. But I had woken to snorting, muttered, "oh—poor thing's hungry," and had gone back to sleep.

I moan a giant-god's name in my sleep, but this is hardly all that queer. Not like the things I've seen with my eyes, the few things others have also seen along with me. The companion who asked who the massive figure was, "leaning into me" like a muse—he saw something. The witch, though—he didn't see anything, not for a little bit, not through the searing pain that doubled him over upon the floor, naked, still erect, shouting useless curses at me. That was pretty queer.

So, too, were the druids who pulled my beard, refusing to let go 'till I pulled theirs back. Queer. Maybe a bit gay.

III.

Who's Brân?

Welsh king. A giant so large "no house could hold him," so massive he laid himself down across a river for troops to cross to the slaughter.

But to know more is where you have to go mad.

I'm trying to world in a god most don't know. Who's Brân? Might as well as who Brad is when you're drunk and naked and trying to remember all the names of the men you've fucked.

Flame like the searing sun and the burning fields magnified in a drop of water falling from a gnarled yew—the dragon, and the giant, and I'm impaled. Him, them, the rock under bare feet, the water raining through him, he's in the world thrust through me.

Brân means Raven in Welsh, or Jackdaw. Jack's a giant killer, climbed a pole of the ancestors to steal back from a giant what'd been stolen. Golden eggs from a goose—there's a druid tale for you, some drunk bards spinning tales of madness because you won't believe what they actually saw.

Raven-men are all over the Welsh lore. Another one, Morfrân, "Great Crow," was a warrior in Arthur's court. (We'll get to that giant-killer in a bit.) Morfrân's also called Afagddu (Utter Darkness), making him in other tales the hideous child of Ceridwen for whom she brewed the potion of Awen, stolen by the boy Gwion "by accident" to become Taliesin. And Afagddu might be a beard-flaying bear.

We know much of this from Taliesin, and Taliesin's a mad liar, awen-drunk poet slipping in and out of time and place to become everything, returning to the "sane" with his tales. There's at least three of him, probably hundreds. He doesn't stay very well in time. Awen will do that you.

So will Brân.

IV.

I woke this morning, remembering being a mountain. I flowed down-river to a city and became king of a people who weren't ready for that sort of king yet.

To learn about a god, you must go mad.

You cannot search for them as you would a job or online date. The internet's only good for all the stuff that we used a post office and a library for. But it's neither a post office nor a library—everything's short, summarized, only what someone thought you'd want to read, as opposed to what someone actually wanted to tell you.

Search for Brân and you get some stuff about the fibrous hull of a grain. In this case, it's not much worse for a Welsh giant gate-keeping god of the dead then it is for Greek gods—ask a search-engine if Apollo really exists and you've got to do some scrolling to get past moon-landing conspiracy sites.

But that's what we think we're left with, which is at least part of the reason why the world's disenchanted, the collective symptom of our shared disease, the one that's infected both this world and Others, the ones where They live, the ones where it makes sense to plant legumes to climb a world-vine to meet a giant or to hang a hundred feet above the ground to talk to one.

We place that disenchantment at different times, the moments of the turning where gods who were present—not just through poets and the mad but to everyone—suddenly withdrew. But this makes sense when we remember that all were not disenchanted at the same time; 'uncontacted' tribes in deep forests still see their spirits. Disenchantment followed dis-in-heritance, displacement from land and forest into factories and mills and offices—it's hard to see a god when you're staring into machines that maul the hands, deafen the ears and dull the eyes with which we sense The Other.

A Kindness of Ravens

That spreading plague started on the same island he's from; the laws passed to midwife in this infestation of desolation came not far from where that giant-killer dug up his head. Now, we've the internet and private property and fizzy sugar water and hand-phones but no gods and this is supposed to be better. This is supposed to be sane.

To be a poet, you must go mad, stoke "fire in the head" searing through shining brows, and steal from Ceridwen's Cauldron the elixir sought for her son Utter-Darkness

Brân had a cauldron, a gift from those he sheltered.

But Irish hospitality's a joke, at least if you're a giant. Two giants lived in Ireland and the Irish built them a house made of iron, then set it on fire to kill them. Didn't work, but the giants didn't retaliate, merely moved across the ocean, over to Wales where Brân welcomed them, let them live anywhere they wanted, unharmed. In return, they gave him their cauldron which would raise the fallen war-dead, the Cauldron of Annwn.

And later another Irish king crosses the water with a war-band, and Brân hosts them, marries off his sister Brânwen to them. To be a good host after his brother maims their horses, Brân gifts them the Cauldron of Annwn, and everything falls apart.

Risen dead, voiceless, are the gifts of that coal-black well, unherded by hounds of the underworld, freed from the rock under which they slept, pouring forth to wage battle on behalf of inhospitable peoples, fueling the machinery of war.

That—*war.*

Mistreatment of his sister sent Brân over-sea as the "swineherds" (some readings suggest "priests") of Ireland saw,

"...a forest on the ocean, where we have never seen a single tree...a great mountain beside the forest, and that was moving; and a soaring ridge on the mountain, and a lake on each side of the ridge."

Brân the giant-king become the land, or Raven the land become the giant-king.

Brân pounds hard into the side of the head, thrusts there with the trunk of an Alder. He is a god of Alder, the warrior of Alder, the wood of shields. A mad poet knew Brân when he saw him:

"The high sprigs of Alder are on thy shield
Brân are thou called, of the glittering branches"

A spear pierced his ankle though maybe also his thigh ("you dogs of Gwern, beware the pierced-thigh"), and most see him as do I—the Fisher-King, hobbled, waiting for the unasked question in a land of desolation.

Here is a land of desolation.

Here is an unasked question.

V.

In dream, he leads me to the edge of a cavern, to the entrance, the gate wood and iron. "I'm moving in to where you live," he says, colors that don't exist exploding around me in those days. "I'll be there, waiting for you on the other side. Don't worry—I'm moving in." And then a druid pulls my beard, hard. And there's the woman I think I recognize but she turns and her face terrifies me. Witches, priests, druids who know something I don't yet know, and then I leave the cavern and he's there, just as he said.

Brân punched a witch pretty hard in the stomach once. He rolled off me, naked, still erect, screaming in pain, holding his abdomen asking what the fuck I'd just done to him. I didn't do a thing, except unconsciously mutter "thanks" to the giant-king I'd suddenly noticed, rescuing a clueless poet from a horrible event he didn't want to be part of.

Brân punches hard, his crows rip flesh, like the Ravens of The Morrígan, stripping dead flesh from crushed bone. And they're on about similar things, I guess, but also not at all, or not yet, and there's that awful war barely repaired and all those dead running loose upon the land.

War's not madness, though. Poetry is. War is machine and sanity, and the sane have trouble with giants. And some giants have trouble with us.

A king comes down from the mountains of Snowdon, from somewhere near where the dragons fought, near where Ceridwen sought the Awen for Afagddu (utter-dark) or Morfrân (great crow) from ancient Fferyllt (alchemists/metal-workers).

From amongst those giants down-river to Harlech comes a king full of giant blood—and what's giant-blood, anyway, but the water that soaks through the mountains into the soul? And there by that lake I saw the giants, there by the lake I saw shimmering dragon-fire, there by the lake I saw Brân.

Some have trouble with giants, and some giants have trouble with us. There was an Arthur, or most likely was. Probably a king in the 5th and 6th century, leading Britons slowly westward as Saxons invaded, leaving finally from Cornwall to Bretagne, what the Romans called Armorica. I saw Brân too in Armorica, by the River called Aulne (Alder), near where a giantess straddled vastly above bird-shit and a wild boar and a drunk dreaming mad poet.

The Welsh translate Satan as Arddu, generally "great darkness." There's a witch-cult who knows an Arddu (pronounced Arthee), which they name as Royal Darkness. Some of what I've heard those witches say about Arddu can also be said of Brân, but witches don't tell many tales to the uninitiated. This protects them, perhaps, but also hides the gods, and giants don't hide. But Arddu's also Arth-du, Dark Bear, and there's a giant-killer's got that name, too.

A few British witch cults know Brân as the "lord of time," in line with Robert Graves. Mining Graves, though, like mining the dead, still leaves you with silent warriors, efficacious but unspeaking. And unraveling Arthur's a fool's game, except for poets even madder still.

Arthur slayed and subdued giants, like factories slay and subdue forests. Giants preferred the beards of men, of kings; sought them out, sheared them from their faces, slayed the resistant ones. Made clothing from them, capes and cloaks and hats, augmented their own beards. Twenty-six lords of Britain all lost their beards and lives to one, 'till Arthur fought him and kept his. Like Jack, Arthur was a rampant giant-slayer, but there was one already dead whom he couldn't slay. From a Welsh Triad:

The Three Concealments:

The Head of Bran Fendigaid, ap Llyr, which was buried in the White Hill in London. and as long as the Head was there in that position, no oppression would ever come to this island

The second: the Bones of Gwerhefyr Fendigaid which were buried in the chief ports of this island

The third: the Dragons which Lludd ap Beli buried in Dinas Emrys in Eryri.

The Three Disclosures:

The Bones (for the love of a woman)

The Dragons by Gwrtheym the Thin

The Head by Arthur because it did not seem right to him that this island should be defended by the strength of anyone other than him.

Still-speaking heads, dead speaking gods shout "Orphic" into the spreadsheets of the sane, but here at least I understand why I found Welsh gods on a druid-mountain in France, if Dark-Bear/Utter-Dark/ Great-Crow took the King of Alder's head across a short channel with him as he fled. That Merlin's Grave, Merlin's Step, and Merlin's Well all sit in the Broceliande (la fôret de Paimpont), in central-west Bretagne, then makes a slight bit more sense.

VI.

I'm staring across a valley at a verdant hill as stormclouds gather in the gloaming evening, staring at a giant wearing a black cloak. He's as tall as the hill behind him, massive, hooded. I can't see his face or his features, only the rippling black fabric covering his form.

There's no wind, but his cloak shakes and then starts to—to fly away, bits of fabric suddenly not fabric but wings, hundreds, thousands, perhaps millions suddenly flying towards me. They're crows—the sky is black with them, and they head past me as I stare at what's left him.

It's only bone, white pillars where once a giant stood.

Here we have the madness now of the poets, of how you know gods.

Brân's a giant. Brân's a raven, or a jackdaw, or a crow. Brân's the Fisher King, guardian of the bleeding lance, wounded in the thigh, waiting for the knight who will ask "the unasked question." The thigh is the groin, the King is barren, his lands in ruins.

In one tale, his name's Bron. In most, Percival doesn't ask, at least not 'till years of further questing to find the grail. In all, the king cannot be healed 'till the question's asked.

Again, that question.

I've had two visions of Brân, both inscrutable. There in the Breton mountains I saw him torn asunder by crows, crows maybe of batttle, crows likely of carrion. And the other, the first, shakes me still, more than the gasping terror as cold fingers clung to the beard of the mountain along a cliff.

I stood alongside one of his bards upon a mountain, looking across to another where settled a people. Grey-black-yellow skies illumined the world below the world as their village was destroyed, flames licking their wood-and-thatch hovels.

And time slipped around us, here in his realm. Settlers survived, built, rebuilt, now with wood and slate that did not withstand another assault.

Again, brick, stone, again fire and destruction, each time the few that remained remembering, rebuilding, rebirthing upon that grand hill.

Until the last, the greatest, towering stone walls and glass and steel, the brilliance of the Fferyllt, the height of humans here arrayed in the sunless realm. And then destruction, and there was no one left to rebuild.

"You understand? "Asked his bard who wore the features I have come to wear. There between us stood silent the unasked question as I nodded and stood before the opening gates of the dead.

The Battle of Trees has Brân opposite Taliesin fighting alongside Arawn, King of the Underworld as champion of those armies, and only dis-closing of his identity from that Alder-shield defeats him. But Taliesin is also at Brân's side invading Ireland. He's one of the seven companions left of the armies of Wales, one of the seven who listens to the head of the giant tell tales and prophesy for decades as they sit out-of-time.

So Brân's a lord of time, then, and Taliesin slips out with him after that battle, and later against him. But Taliesin was also the boy Gwion, accidentally stealing the three drops of Awen meant for Morfrân Giant Crow, for Afaggdu Utter-Darkness. And to obliterate finally all sanity from the soil of our soul, Taliesin leads the Dark Bear-King into Annwn to gain there the Cauldron brought by giants.

Here madness takes us if we hope to know Brân, but here sanity should flee us if we hope to survive.

It is perfectly sane to wage out your time in work, to wage war fueled by the coal-black-blood of the unspeaking dead. It is madness to live free, to love forests, to slip out of time with gods.

From Ceridwen's Cauldron came the Awen, and those who'd drank it became mad. Speaking of the Awenyddion, a traveler in 1194 said:

> "There are certain persons in Cambria, whom you will find nowhere else, called Awenyddion, or people inspired; when consulted upon any doubtful event, they roar out violently; are rendered beside themselves, and become, as it were, possessed by a spirit."
>
> Giraldus Cambrensis, Description of Wales

I know that madness. It spun through my being while climbing a rock-face to ask giants for help to re-awaken Brân into the world; it rips through my soul in panicked moments when a god's trying to say something my small human brain is too rigid to comprehend, when suddenly you cannot stop writing until every last boiling bit of the Otherworld is wrung out of you.

The madness of the Awen-struck is the madness of the land. Taliesin shifts not only through time but through place and through beings, both in the chase of Ceridwen's rage at the theft of Awen and in *The Battle of Trees*, where Alder leads in the fray, where Brân is unveiled as the warrior of the Dead.

And then *The Hostile Confederacy*:

> *I have been a course, I have been an eagle.*
> *I have been a coracle in the seas:*
> *I have been compliant in the banquet.*
> *I have been a drop in a shower;*
> *I have been a sword in the grasp of the hand*
> *I have been a shield in battle.*
> *I have been a string in a harp,*
> *Disguised for nine years.*
> *in water, in foam.*

The madness of Awen is the becoming of everything, slipping through time, inhabiting place, becoming the spirits of the land and the land itself.

And it was there after the giants, after spirit in the river, after the hound at the gate, I drenched the rain soaking the mountains into giant-blood towards the sea.

The sea is everywhere, the rain soaks everyone, and giants do not sit still.

VII.

Brân is a giant, a lord of time, a god of witches, a warrior of the dead, a king in the wastes, and is the dragon of the land.

In *Branwen fearch Llyr*, the Irish swineherds see the land itself rise against them, but this is no surprise.

We cannot blame the Irish king Matholwch for the war which brought a land against him, but rather his people. All through the tale of Brân, King Matholwch pleads for peace. He first housed the giants who brought Brân the Cauldron of the Dead, 'till his people, disgusted, demanded an iron house be built to immolate them. It is the people who demand Brânwen's demeaning in the kitchen, and his people who plot to slaughter the giant in his sleep.

Here, then, the unasked question, as desolation spread outward from the city where laid buried Brâns head, disclosed so that no land-god might be relied upon for protection. From London spread the greatest plague known to us, far more virulent than the pox and Black Death, displacing peoples, disenchanting villages, destroying the forests. Mountains tumble-down upon the lakes to disclose the black-coal dead, pumpjack giant-killers siphon from the earth the blood of Annwn.

And the people cry out to the kings: what need we of gods when we have machines? What need we of a lord of time when we measure it out in hourly wages? What need we of kings when we can kill giants? What need we of madness when sanity is everywhere?

To understand a god, you must become mad. To understand madness, you must become a poet.

And here's where the maddest of them all, that Awen-thief bard slipping out of time and becoming everything, who fought alongside Brân and yet unveiled him, who stole from Ceridwen's cauldron and yet helped win it, who fled from the vengeance of a goddess and yet was birthed from he, can unravel one final secret.

VIII.

Multiple gods-bothered folk have made connections between giants in Celtic and the chthonic powers of the land. It's tempting to ascribe this same connection to Brân, but for a problem—Brân leaves Wales, rising up as trees, mountains and lakes across the Irish Sea to rescue his sister. Brân is not merely the land, but embodies the land and its power; the land comes with and through him.

A god shows up; people see Alder. It is the same with each Welsh god I've seen; Arianrhod is there in the shifting of light through grey-and-blue-and-violet clouds and sky reflected in water, her magic pouring from the land into the soul. In Snowdon, the lake where sought Ceridwen the ritual of Awen soaks her into your boots as you step, as giants shake rain from their shrub-beards.

Here, again, the unasked question of disenchantment. Western European societies stopped seeing the giants shaking their shrub-beards precisely at the time they began extracting the coal from their hearts to power machines to wage time into money and nature into commodity. It became "sane" and rational to enclose land, build factories, and mete out human time according to the clocks of the Capitalist, and "madness" to slip between those hedges, sabotage the machines, and slip out-of-time.

At the end of *The Battle of Trees* are three strange lines; Taliesin is not here to explain them (though on this fact I'd not wage my madness):

> *I am splendid*
> *And shall be wanton*
> *From the oppression of the metal-workers.*

A land rises up through a god through the re-enchantment of a bard against "the oppression of the metal-workers." The Welsh is Fferyll, perhaps the Fferyllt who held enchained in words the recipe for Awen. Taliesin's the thief there, but perhaps Ceridwen is too, manifesting from herbs, fire, and water what was locked in words, the secret of enchantment.

It is that secret we need now, awakened forests waging war, trees taking sides against each other while a mad bard dances through time and place; similar somewhat to what Lugh gains from his witches in *The Second Battle of Tadgh Mor*:

> *"And ye, O Be-cuile and O Dianann," said Lugh to his two witches, "what power can ye wield in the battle?"*
>
> *"Not hard to tell," said they. "We will enchant the trees and the stones and the sods of the earth, so that they shall become a host under arms against them, and shall rout them in flight with horror and trembling."*

Brân is both the land and the god clothed in land, a giant lumbering in form of forests again against those who've stolen from the dead as in *The Battle of the Trees*, and the great Alder-shield who, awakened by our poetic madness, leads first amongst the warriors of the land against the oppression of the metal-workers, the giant-killing machines, and the desolation of disenchantment.

After The Fire,
Invisible

Because I'm drunk I'm thinking
If I ever fall in love with whoever you are
and you, poor fool, fall for that old trick too.
And then later, after sheets strewn with
feathers and hide from some poor beast
who died to give us pleasure, like that one guy

who died to clean up our sins but missed a few spots

if after those sheets somehow still on the bed
and perhaps broken plaster, we ever
put on our armor again, thumbing passports
at the back of immigration lines, you in a city
reclaimed from the sea, and me? a raised swamp
or wet valed mountains where I'll bury my skull

and we decide, because love is best when it ends
in glory, not in tears, and feathers and anyway
I forget why we're talking on love

She Sends A Flood Upon The World

because I still haven't learned how to breathe
through you or to even hear your voice past
what you say, to what they never hear

Oh! *Sorry.* Across oceans, stern women checking our papers
which are like feathers and sheets, unstrewn
unlike the words I'm always leaving around
after we were fools and fell in love, and picked ourselves up
from such silly endeavors, perhaps we can part not here
but there, some third port neither yours nor mine

not because I know how this goes, or even what we do

with all those feathers we're collecting in cities
where we'll only find more, and shrug, thinking
that all our talk of love was too serious for our souls
a third port, please, because my city and yours
should always wait away, so we can end this
before it ever began, know where we leave off

the final pages of the book I told you I wouldn't read
running ahead long before I even said words
you're warning me not to mean. And anyway, I can never
be your sweat-soaked shirt as you run. That was silly
because I meant only, I'd like to feel your sweat
soaking into me, leaving feathers, worn leather

at an airport, somewhere far, but neither mine–
as I leave back into forward, the plan all along–or yours
and you become what you ought.
Perhaps I helped, maybe, you'll think, standing at that window
like the beautiful way you buy yoghurt (I'll never tell)
and perhaps I helped too.

Why were we talking of love, when what I'd meant to say
and you are obscured in memory, like that dream
and that other, and I start to wonder why you're here?
But you're also there, and so am I, across an ocean, waiting
for strange men to check our names and dreams
to see if we are worthy.

You know this is really bad poetry, but I'm drunk, and
as I said, I was thinking, that when we finally leave
(if that isn't now—I cannot tell)
it be in some third port, because we got talking of love
but you don't yet know that I hate, more than anything
her voice, reminding, that you cannot smoke

And all the names, expertly pronounced, who are not yet
at the gate, taking them from those they do not know
or do, their stories aren't ours, but there they are
Hayakawa, Abdul, Gerhardt and Smith, but all you
really want is to smoke, but you can't, because she said
two minutes ago, and two minutes from now

And more names, and you're not staying, nor is their plane
except for a moment, "you are delaying the flight,"
and all they want is a cigarette.
Like me, there, in that place where you'll likely go, and I
elsewhere, holding a passport in hand, and
feather in pocket, or in ear.

We were talking on love, and that's too serious for
what we'll eventually do, part over oceans in boxes
where you cannot smoke, or dream,
but it doesn't matter, because that's everything after.
"You are delaying the flight," she says, and I
say *fuck you let them smoke*, because maybe

I should really tell you what I mean.
If we don't part now, then for the love of gods
and feathers, and sweat-soaked shirts, then fuck
don't make me say good-bye at Schiphol.
I'll not delay your flight, but you should know
we should leave elsewhere, if not here, because

I really fucking hate that fucking airport.

Dahut At The Floodgates

Aranrot drem clot tra gwawr hinon,
Mwyhaf gwarth y marth o parth Bryth(r)on:
Dysbrys am y llys efnys afon,
Afon a'e hechrys gwrys gwrth terra,
Gwenwyn y chynbyt kylch byt ed a.

Aranrot whose beauty surpasses the radiance of dawn,
Her terrifying was the greatest shame by means of a wand.
A hostile river rushes about her court,
A river that assaults and injures the land,
Venom of the old world that circles the world.

(Kadeir Kerrituen/The Chair of Ceridwen)

I. What the Anarchist Saw

"It's fucking awesome there's an anti-Capitalist Pagan event in Olympia."
I looked at the guy who said this, a local, not a named polytheist by any
means, no one you probably know. And then I looked around to see who

72

else had heard his enthusiasm, to see if someone else would correct him instead of me. I was exhausted, tired of words, my arm tired from carrying a shield no one could see.

But there was no one there to tell him otherwise, so it fell on me. After-all, I was the one he'd spoken to.

"Uh–it's not really an anti-capitalist conference. There are some here, yeah, but it's a Polytheist event."

He looked like he thought I was joking. "Polytheists are all anti-Capitalists and anarchists, though…"

I shook my head, noticing a few people I'd previously run afoul of regarding money-in-paganism standing nearby. "No, not–"

And then I smiled, remembering what I'd been seeing all weekend. "They are. Just don't tell them that."

II. Leather, Wet From the Dragon's Well

My boots were wet again. They were wet like the last time, though there'd been no rain. In fact, the heat in Olympia that weekend was brutal; the air-conditioning couldn't keep up, but the building wasn't old enough to have been constructed before conditioned air was a thing at all. Tall, square, soaking up the light and heat from the unseely summer torching our ancient forests, filled with sweltering gods-folk barely complaining.

In fact–no one was complaining, or not really. There were some snags, though. The hotel manager obviously didn't like people, probably had hoped to be a good Capitalist instead of a servant of Capitalists. He treated some of us awfully, but the rolled-eyes of his staff hinted at a fierce class-war enacted behind the desk. As everywhere, the people actually doing work, rather than telling others to do work, were quite awesome.

And they wouldn't have noticed my sopping-wet boots, because they left no puddle, no moisture. Only I could feel the leather wet from the chill waters of Llyn Dinas, and know I was elsewhere again.

This has happened before. A few times just before the conference, sitting in a scorched field feeding crows as I cried for something I realized couldn't exist; once after, just as I was contemplating whether I could write any of this. One particular time in February, when a would-be king spewed words even he couldn't believe he'd said, as the waves of Llyn Dinas lapped against the carpet of another hotel room.

My boots were wet again, as was the rest of me, face down in muck as a great army tread across my body to another shore.

Just before Many Gods West, I'd undergone some of the most terrifying transformations. I do not have the words for them; even poetry fails. I don't know if it's a story I can ever tell, except to the few who guided me back out of the Abyss, as well as one to whom all these events eventually led. They ended all at once, a sprinkling of soil as fire coursed through my body and a shield, lit by candleflame, awoke within me as I awoke within it, and that thunderous laughter coming from below and behind yet still shaking through my parched throat.

A mystery that started on the shores of Llyn Dinas, seared through with a burning lance of light from within the Dagda's home, finally became the Wheel and the World, and my boots were wet all weekend.

III. The Gates of the Dead Rattle

Others' boots were wet, from lake water nearer-by. When one attendee arrived, he hurried to the shores of the drowned shanty-town to attend to the dead. Others shook in ancestral terror after a ritual, the dead we carry with us suddenly both lighter yet more real.

The dead are everywhere in Olympia. The city sits upon a fault, just near the epicenter of the quake whose damage is still not fully repaired in Seattle, 90 miles North. The giants are everywhere, too, and water pours freely and fiercely from a spring in the middle of the city, like those of the ancient European cities where our gods were most worshiped.

And there were gate-keepers for them, or rather, gate-openers. Sean Donahue is the most gentle giant of a man you might ever meet, yet wherever he stands there is also a gate of the dead, a power too many witches claim and too many more desire. To gain access to the realms of the dead is to gain power, and witchcraft and Paganism is too much about power. Therein's also why polytheists are so hated, so belittled, and so feared–because they yet care nothing for power, and stab through the heart those who would rise above the others.

I'm getting ahead of myself, and painting this broad and macabre, but there are no brighter shades with which to hue this dying world. When the Mothers arrived in ritual the third day of the conference, they laughed as they said the same gods-damned thing we've already heard from all the other gods: a storm's coming.

We know, because they've told us. Some fear the apocalyptic vision of the gods-folk, in the same way they deride Peter Grey's manifesto without ever having touched the thing. Apocalypse is for the Christians, or the fools, or those who hate others, or those who hate themselves. But if you do not care for a world, than you will not care that it dies, anymore than you'll notice the slaughtered Black folk in American streets until you decide they're worth caring about.

That "storm" is like the dying city the Singers in the Darkness showed me, or the Ragnorak heard by some in the Troth, not some mere windy day when electricity clips for a few hours and we're forced to stare into our own darkness, but the relentless slaughter of the world. But unlike the New Agers or the Christians, no polytheist I've met believes some magical figure or change of consciousness will be born from the withered husk of what we call the world. Each vision is more dour and dire than the next, the sense of urgency quickening, and a panic settling into a new routine of conserving water, saying good-bye to great mammals, and chastising ourselves for ever needing to travel.

The Mothers laughed and said it again, "a storm is coming," and it seemed so predictable that it was a bad joke, and yet the threads they weave and cut are deadly serious.

IV. Knives in Streets as Forests Burn

The hotel had never endured such heat, the staff apologizing, the air conditioning unable to keep up with the 160 folks gathered to hear Morpheus Ravenna speak. Polytheists are anarchists whether they care to be or not–we'd run out of chairs in the room, before I finished asking for help gathering more 6 people rushed passed me into the other room to carry stacks of them back. None were paid to find seats for others, none waiting to be called specifically, merely a need to be met and a rush to meet it.

Stained-glass windows and light, the clothing of the gods; I felt almost I'd heard some of those words before, said better by her than ever by the fumbling poet who'd tried a year ago. This happened a few times, hearing words I'd tried to capture from echoing forests spoken by friends or strangers. We'd heard the same echo, caught the same threads, pulled strands to weave the tapestries of the worlds around us, the worlds with gods in it, the worlds inhabiting a dying, scorching, quaking earth.

The dead lingered on the shores of an artificial lake, the pillars of the earth uneasy, unsettled below us. Far to the west, forests climbing the face of the gods' mountain smouldered, a rainforest parched, the last great ancestral towers of this land alight in flame.

When the Mothers spoke of the storm, they laughed; they certainly know we already knew. That's why we were all there, so many of us from across the land, reluctantly riding carbon-spewing death machines through the air and across asphalt to speak on such things, to be near others with similar visions, to be near others to whom gods speak.

Stormcrows winged black-feathered flight through the words. Another mentioned it first: a narrative, a story unfolding from each speech. His on the millenarian Chinese, the revolts led by gods and heretics gathering the poor and trampled against rulers thought divine. It seemed familiar, he said so, we spoke of a story unfolding, each speaker weaving a melody out of the notes of the previous.

And something was inescapable about these presentations. I alternating between two utterly different speakers, Finnchuill and Heimlich A. Laguz, one speaking on Becoming Placed, the other on Heathen Cosmology, and yet as I left one in mid-sentence to check on the other, it was difficult to separate the two. One spoke of disenchantment, the other spoke of disen-chantment; one referenced the capitalist un-godding of the land, the next referenced the same, just in different words.

Rituals for the dead, workshops for the dead. A purging ritual, a warrior ritual. Recovering the monsters, becoming the monsters, slipping between genders, slipping between worlds. It was rare not to hear a reference to the slaughter of Black folk in American streets, or the slaughtering of the forests, or the severing of our meaning, and in at least two presentations (including mine), these were all noted as springing from the same putrid source.

V. No King But Ludd...

So when the Anarchist lauded the event an an anti-capitalist, anarchist Pagan conference, it was dishonest of me to deny this.

I was wearing the same shirt as many others there, Alley Valkyrie's mis-chievous artistic coup. At the Polytheist Leadership Conference last year (the direct ancestor to Many Gods West), we were all wearing her bees, as she'd sent them as her offering to the event. You'd think we were all some cult of apiarists, all devotees of the Melissa, but as Chakrabarty points out, academics miss the point when studying polytheists. It matters not the shape of our belief; rather, it's our practice which worlds them into the earth, and so the PLC became devoted to bee-goddesses, and Many Gods West was an Anarchist event.

A Kindness of Ravens

No Masters, says the second half of the slogan, and it's actually this very thing (and not the worship of multiple gods) that sets the polytheists out from the rest of Paganism. Who are our rockstars? Our elders? Our regents?

We have none, because we thus far topple them.

The moment someone begins to claim power-over, we cut into their breasts and throw their nipples and body into the bog, because we'll have no High Priests, no Kings, no Temple-school gay triads of publishing empires and empty promises and selfies taken in the asphalt court of a San Jose Starbucks.

That is, if we remember where that path leads.

Consider: In a few months in New Orleans a business-owner and marketing quean will host a high-priced event, despite having outed the legal identities of women and exhorted them to call out his name while they're being raped. There's money to be made, and influence to be had–we should not be surprised that several famous witches didn't withdraw from this event, protesting that "we should all just get along." In Brand-Named Paganism, the coin is all, and we can always claim oppression to rally the faithful, just like Evangelicals–and shut down any dissent that gets in the way.

A polytheist who tried that shit currenly would be publicly disembowled before being thrown from a cliff to be fed to the carrion-eaters, and as harsh as this might seem to bourgeois 'let's all get along' Paganism, it's a lot less harsh than the circling of power seen in the Covenant of the Goddesses' response regarding Black lives. That anyone still reads so-called elders after their defense of racism should appall anyone but a Catholic apologist for pedophile priests, because they (and the self-proclaimed Kings) are playing at the same game.

This sort of polytheism is a revolt, regardless the politics of individual gods-bothered folks. An uprising both against the people who defend awful people just because they're Pagan, and an insurgency against those who'd argue we keep our heads down, be good workers, and choke down the shit-covered cock of Liberal Capitalism. It's as much the *Apocalyptic Witchcraft* of Peter Grey as the loom-breaking of the soldiers of King Ludd.

I can only hope it will stay that way.

VI. Exclusively-Priced Tours of the Otherworld

Why bother calling out the merchant-witches, the ticket-sellers at the Gates, the money-changers in the temples? Precisely this: they are, more than anyone, the would-be Authority of Pagan belief, extracting tithes from the seekers of magic, barring the way of those who do not proffer money for a chance to see the Otherworld. It is they who would codify, they who would build the temples only if they might become the High Priests.

Thus far, we fear and tear down the institutions of Paganism both because we'd otherwise be institutionalized, and because we don't need Authority. We may let some leaders around, mostly because they do good stuff, but when the time comes for them to abdicate, we're ready with our pitchforks if they won't.

Who are the masters of the gods-bothered? The gods themselves, and they are myriad, and are more often waiting for us to open the gates to the DisEnchanted Kingdom in cover of darkness so they can wreak their havoc, torch the plastic edifice and loot the treasuries stolen first from the graves. The Dead rattle at the gates, and we're letting them in, dancing with them through the plague-ridden streets of the cities already crumbling.

You may think this dire, perhaps even violent, but only because you do not look past the razor-wire border fences to our south, or the obliteration of indigenous peoples on the land we inhabit, or the blown-off faces of Muslim children in eastern deserts. That's violent. This is compassion, the other edge of the sword of love.

The brutality of the gods-bothered is the severity of their hope, the madness of their poetry is a love letter to the world, and for that weekend I bore a shield atop a quaking fault in a city of the gods.

What Brân asked of me was what was needed, laying face-down in a cold rushing river as others trampled my back across to the other side. I don't believe I'll be here for the next Many Gods West; I think my path lies across a larger body of water, the direction my own skull will one day face in burial unclear to me.

But I do not not think my struggle will be for much longer on these colonized shores, nor against those happily clinging to their cars and corporations, more so in the name of 'witchcraft.'

Amusingly, perhaps, there were two intentional hexes on MGW, a third accidental but no less troublesome. Still more lesser ill-will from those fearful of the gates we're opening. What the gods-bothered are doing is what the respectables warned for decades against–we're refusing to shut up. The gods cannot be secret, their teachings cannot be hidden. Some have cut narrow paths through the forests of the Other and hidden the way; others wider paths with signs and wayside shrines.A few have found great clearings, picked up rusty axes to appear responsible, and now charge a steep toll for their stolen knowledge.

To many of them, what we were doing that first weekend in August was a danger, an offense. If gods are real, anyone can know them. Their secret cults and training courses become irrelevant when you don't need their gatekeeping to meet them, only a little help to learn to hear them. Riverboat cruises with over-glamoured celebrities are meaningless when the Dead will whisper greater secrets to you in rainy gloaming streets, and charms of summoning and binding are no better than the battery cages of factory farms.

Polytheists won't fucking shut up about their gods, gods that witch traditions have long hoped to keep secret and exclusive so to glean and gain their power. But power for what, really?

Power to start a witch-cult with your two sexual partners and build glossy websites and post a selfie to thousands of adoring Facebook likes?

To work the pillaging Market to your favor and comfort?

Power to gain sex, or celebrity, or to make your business prosper?

Those who'd opened gates to the Other have been charging admission, forgetting that other gates can be thrown open, the doors ripped off the hinges, the Other flooding through.

And already I've seen the gilded glint in the eyes of some of the gods-bothered, and I understand Dahut, fingering the key to the floodgates.

VII. She Sends A Flood Over The World

I learned to unravel hexes not from some class or book, but from asking a few gods to teach me to do so. Nagas swept in from the sea to aid one of us, a few giants sloshing through those deep waters to offer their help, as giants are so often wont to do. The Kami blessed this thing because we asked them, not because we deserved it. The dead, the ancestors, the land itself all listened to our call, not because we were powerful, but because we weren't trying to use them like petroleum or slaves.

And not using things like petroleum or slaves is precisely what should've been written in our doctrines, not "do as thou wilt" or 'an it harm none,' but "overthrow the rich and bring the forests back." The pleasant cottage witch poisons the landlord, the kind village elder arms the rebels. That we applaud ourselves for crafting a statement on the environment more pro-Capitalist than the Pope's reveals how far "an it harm none" has gotten us.

Things are breaking open, and this will not be pretty, and this will not be pleasant, and we have little say in the matter anymore.

The gods will show up to whom they will, more so than even those who've shepherded us this far will be able to track. And they will not look like us, and they may not be known as gods, except in the howling slaughter of a Carnivalesque uprising, the dead dancing through those gates we can no longer keep shut.

In fact, the strongest movements–like the best leaders, wisely destroy themselves. They throw themselves face-down into river-fords, they slice off the lips of horses and climb solemnly into the Cauldron, they laugh whimsically while caressing the levers of the floodgates.

All these things said of Polytheism will one day become untrue, if it does not first implode itself back into the raw earth and ancient forests, its gods-maddened heretics stumbling back into the cities with sharpened blades, poison roots, and feral visions of what the flooding torrents and lightning-scorched earth can become.

The Polytheists may one day become the new flaccid elders, searching for relevance, trolling for fresh voices to add to their empires, for influence, for power, and for the sacred coin, and three decades from now shake their heads at the new upstarts clamoring for revolution, hearing voices, wielding strange magics we thought we'd locked up behind gates.

All those clamouring for grip upon the flimsy "Pagan umbrella," the older and venerable witch-cults, have failed to learn what the gods-bothered must:

There can be no Authority, there can be no complicity, there can be no Capital, there can be no Masters.

Peter Grey's done better than I ever might to outline these failings, the diminishing of our danger in order to be respectable, the compromises with Capital while the earth withers around us. But even then, we needed none to show us this, only someone to say what we stopped letting ourselves say, to ask what we stopped allowing ourselves to ask.

We can all become this Jetzt-zeit, the gods-bothered leading the way, even as we are already this.

Or we can all stand pushing for space beneath a flimsy umbrella, a hastily thrown-together field-tent as the rains begin, hoping to be the center of attention, the center of a dying world.

The aluminum frame's about to break, the plastic tent-poles are bending and soon broken. Soon, the people who'd been hoping for a weekend-social or a little comfort will be soaked, and we with them, as lightning streaks across darkened skies.

The gates above and the gates below have opened, and nothing can hold back the flood.

Not even us.

The Roots of Our Resistance

I stood in the street-front garden on a languid August evening. The sun had set, the heavy Friday commuter traffic dwindled on the arterial street before me, a pause of quiet settling over the city before the raging hoards of week-end revelers awoke to earlier memories of life.

The gloaming light faded just as the street-lamps ignited, shining amberic yellow across the concrete stones radiating the last of the day's heat into the cooling night. I breathed in, deeply, taking in the intoxicating scents around me. Nicotiana filled the heavy, thick drunk air as I unraveled the garden hose, my bare feet brushing against chamomile and mint. I opened the spigot, directing a slow spray of water on the baked-earth in which nasturtium, Victorian lilac, and heather rooted amongst human-high blades of vetiver and taller-still sunflower.

Nothing ready to harvest those weeks in August; all the greens had long-before gone to seed, and the tomatoes and peppers not yet ready. I liked that time of year best, in between one harvest and the next, my garden planned to explode in heady blossoms while vegetables and roots swelled pregnant in the long heat.

This was my home, a shared house in the middle of the city in the Capitol Hill neighborhood of Seattle, then still an enclave of queers, artists, urban service workers, hipsters, and old Black families sharing the same streets and cafes in the 10 blocks near my garden. One of the first neighborhoods established on the forested hills, ancient trees still winning out over perpetually cracked concrete, centuries-old roots throwing off asphalt and brick with easy indifference.

The house was built early in the 1900s, but I was much newer to it, having moved just after the WTO protests in the last year of the last century. The neighborhood was gorgeous, playful, the spirits and animals curious and kind, the side-streets as much a foot-path as the sidewalks, alleys hiding mysteries, swelling with quiet contentment. It was a good place, all I needed and wanted of a neighborhood, a city, a world.

That night I stood outside to water my garden somewhat distracted. Several things weighed on mind, particularly the increasing costs of living where I did. The neighborhood was in upheaval, that slow war of gentrification and displacement, increasing costs without increasing wages. The rent on our place had not yet gone up, but all the other expenses were becoming difficult to manage on my full-time social work income, even after sharing the burden of rent, utilities and food with my lover and roommates.

My lover was inside at the time, with another lover. I'd wanted to give them some time to each other, and I'd wanted to stand in the garden. I'd suspended candle lanterns from the branches of an elder tree another lover had rescued 6 year before, other lanterns swayed from wrought-iron sections of fence we'd found in alleyways and converted into trellises for climbing cathedral bells, morning-glories, and black-eyed susan vine. Amongst those planted vines, ivy—cut back years before—crept back to war with a rather resilient clematis, and amongst those candles and vines, wild lupine and scotch broom and opium poppy peeked through, each flower and shrub and vine a story, each planting of it a relic of my life always ready to be re-lived.

I sat for awhile, perhaps over-watered, lingering, wondering if they'd had enough time alone, wondering if I should make maybe take tea in the garden. It was a beautiful night—all options seemed pleasurable, all paths leading towards contentment. I'd decided on tea, but just as I turned, I heard my neighbors' voice call out.

"Hey! You got a transfer?" he asked. I turned, glad to see him. We'd known each other for over a decade, and he'd been there long before I'd arrived. At 15 years in my home, I was a newcomer—he'd lived there his entire 45 years, which were short compared to his grandmother's 96 years.

"Yeah," I said, digging the paper bus ticket from my over-full pockets.

We had an illegal trade going. He started it a decade ago, running across the street to hand me a crumbled purple ribbon of newsprint, an unexpired bus transfer. I'll admit, a stranger running at you, shouting, as you wait for a bus is a bit startling, and I was probably awfully defensive that first time.

"Don't pay," he'd said, stopping in front of me. "I got a transfer."

At first I'd refused. Metro transfers are non-transferable, and I was more a liberal then, and less the anarchist. I imagined it my moral duty to pay for public transit, regardless of how poor I was. But the man was nice, and he'd sprinted a hundred feet across a busy street to give me a free ride, so I accepted.

That act started our long friendship. Whenever I'd see him, I'd say hello, and offer him any unexpired transfers that I had if he was waiting at the stop. Sometimes he'd leave his on the sign-post by the bus shelter, and then I started doing that, too.

My large balcony overlooked the street and the bus stop, and I'd sometimes spot him offer used transfers to others, too. Most would refuse, particularly the well-dressed white women, and I'd sigh sadly, watching their body language show their fear or disgust of the large Black man trying to save them a couple of dollars.

That evening, I handed him mine—an 'owl' transfer, good until the next morning. I also offered him a cigarette, though he hadn't asked. I enjoyed his company, despite always forgetting his name. He always forgot mine, too, no matter how many times we'd offer them to each other. After most of a decade of talking, laughing, sharing a beer or sprinting across a busy street to save the other guy a few dollars, names really didn't matter as much as everything else.

We stood outside together, talking, watching the street lamps flicker and the increasing weekend traffic begin to flood the street. My mind was still a bit distracted by my lover's guest inside, though not from jealousy. The man inside was a writer, too, a left-leaning journalist for a local alternative paper, who'd written several articles about this recent wave of gentrification in our neighborhood. We didn't agree on much—he saw the changes as good and inevitable; I saw them as horrifying as my steady income seemed to pay for less and less each month. We'd talked amiably about it, though, but the matter weighed on me.

In the garden, I asked my neighbor, my co-conspirator against the rising cost of public transit, a question I'd been meaning to ask for several months. As he'd lived in his home his entire life, and his grandmother was the first to live in their century-old house, I figured he'd have some insight.

I'd wanted to know how he'd fared during the sub-prime era a few years before, when predatory mortgage brokers would go door-to-door trying to get poorer families to take out equity loans or to sell their home altogether.

"Hey," I asked. "Did you and your grandmother ever get hit by the loan sharks a couple of years ago?"

"Shit," he'd said, dragging his cigarette, one eye scanning the street for the bus. "We still do, and the real estate agents. There was a woman here just yesterday–she comes by every week trying to get my grandma to sell."

I probably looked a bit stupid from the shock. His grandmother was almost a hundred years old, suffering from age-related dementia, could barely remember her own name let alone make such a decision.

He told me he had to chase another out of his house a month before—his grandmother had let the real estate agent in while he was gone, and by the time he'd arrived his grandmother was already fumbling with a pen to sign away the home she'd been born into. He'd torn those papers up in a fury and pushed the woman out.

A house next to us had sold for almost a million dollars a few years before, after its owner had paid my landlord and another to cut down trees to increase the view from its windows onto Lake Washington and the Cascade mountains. I never learned how much my landlord was paid, but I rued their loss every summer when the heat in my second-story room became so unbearable I could rarely sleep before 5am.

The house next to my friend's rented for six thousand dollars a month, the house on the other side of him had sold and was being torn down for new apartments. The hyper-inflated market for housing in a dense and vibrant neighborhood offered quite the buy-out for those whose desire for money outweighed their sense of place and ties to their home. For him, though, despite being employed only part-time while caring for his very elderly grandmother, it made no sense to sell and move from the house built by his great grandfather.

He told me there'd been plenty of times he was tempted when the electricity was about to go out because of unpaid bills. Worse, several of the mortgage brokers pitched hard–he was in his mid-forties and had never owned a car, never traveled. A mortgage or a sale would mean he could buy a car and wouldn't need to bus all the time, wouldn't need to trade transfers with his neighbor to make ends meet.

Making a Killing

You might not know the scam here, particularly if you are white—I was ignorant of this myself until about a decade ago.

Black home-owners are continuously targeted by real estate agents and predatory lenders in neighborhoods primed for "urban renewal" (that is, gentrification). Because they're minorities, their plight and position elicits little sympathy and solidarity from the middle-class white liberals who dominate the politics in many cities, and their high unemployment rates often mean they are more likely to endure long periods of poverty. They also have less access to the lines of credit freely offered to middle-class whites.

But many of them owned homes, particularly in areas that were once considered poor and undesirable neighborhoods. And for families like my friend's, the home was theirs, long-ago paid off or never borrowed for in the first place. Without income, though, and without easy credit, the house becomes the only thing they can draw from, and banks are too-often willing to take a house as collateral on an 'equity loan.'

There are many ways a loan can go wrong, the most obvious one being that jobs are lost or medical crises ensue, and the failure to repay that loan (often for relatively small amounts compared to the value of the house) means everything is lost.

Because we live in a racist, capitalist Democracy, profit is the only religion and any problems you endure are considered your own responsibility, even if those problems were caused by manipulative land speculators and bankers composing confusing loan agreements. And speculators often target Black home owners because they know they are poor, often strapped for cash, less educated than their white neighbors, and their lack of political power means their complaints are often ignored or considered hysteria by those outside their communities.

Mortgage brokers and loan officers (who, like real estate agents are often paid on commission) see Black home-owners as easy targets, particularly since the pay-off for a loan default is often extra-ordinarily high compared to the amount lent. During the sub-prime mortgage crisis, when interest rates were low and regulation was lax, brokers and real estate agents targeted Black home owners particularly, approving loans with variable rates (often interest rates that tripled after a year of repayment), making a "killing" in new housing markets.

A Kindness of Ravens

During the heady days of the 'sub-prime' mortgages, it seemed I couldn't go anywhere without hearing about the new rage in home ownership from friends and strangers. Everyone wanted to get in on "flipping," where you buy a house, hold it for a year or two, and sell it for $50- to $100 thousand more than your original loan, pocketing the difference as profit.

"In fact," a long-time friend of mine explained after he flipped his first house, "you wouldn't have to work for others anymore. Rhyd–you could write while fixing up a house. And they don't care how much money you're making now–they'll give a loan to anyone. You'd be stupid not to."

Lax regulation, high unemployment, and government policies to push home ownership as the American Dream created an overheated engine of profit for those who did the transfers. And each sale meant a little more profit, and many people were buying only to sell again, with no interest in the communities they bought homes in.

It all seemed really, really wrong…and it was.

A friend got caught on his second house as the market collapsed, and he, along with many, many other people, were all 'underwater' (owing more on their loans than the resale value of their houses). But worse than the obvious game and great forgetting of everyone involved (they, like me, had witnessed the "dot com" bubble in Seattle, after all), was the fact that this shell game was being played at the expense of poor and Black folk, who lost their homes in droves when the money they'd borrowed to pay down medical debt, perform long-needed repairs, or get them through an economic rough-patch couldn't be paid back. They lost not only the roofs over their heads, but also the decades and almost centuries of rootedness that came from living in the same home as your ancestors.

And in the last 6 years, another round of the shell-game had begun in our city and our neighborhood. Large internet technology companies had begun expanding their profit-ventures and needed more workers to help them do it. Traditionally Black and gay neighborhoods became war zones again, threatening to push both him and I out in favor of a whiter, straighter population.

Ancestral Trauma and the Cycle of Violence

The ancestors of many Black folk in America were hauled from their homes in chains in the hulls of ships, becoming an uncompensated labor force to subdue the colonized lands of the Americas. From one great break of ancestry to another, the descendents of folks living on the continent of Africa found their traditions severed by the ravenous lust of Capital both through slavery and through the pillaging of land speculation.

Marxist historians speak of a process called Primitive Accumulation, [Primitive as in primary or initial, not as in the "opposite of civilized,"] the plundering of natural resources (wood, minerals, people). This accumulation usually involved violence: the Crusades, imperial conquest of South America, and slave-taking were all acts of Primitive Accumulation, and all resulted in great wealth for European rulers and merchants. That initial accumulation of wealth at the point of the sword then became the wealth that we now call Capital.

Primitive Accumulation caused massive displacements of people and destruction of societies—the deaths from conquest in the Americas and the hauling of humans in chains across oceans being obvious examples. But this way of gaining wealth is never very sustainable–one can only plunder so many ancient cities of their gold and people before there's no longer any gold or people left to plunder.

Capitalism is a more systematic and efficient method of plunder, as it invests those stolen resources into localized cycles of oppression. Consider: the effort to hire an army willing to risk death to conquer another people for its wealth is intense, requiring state sanction and ideological support (the Crusades, the War on Terror)–and this method is usually only available to kings. For lesser lords (and their descendents, the 'Bourgeoisie'), it was easier to exploit the people around them rather than traveling overseas.

But Capitalism operates, still, on the same logic as primitive accumulation—the 'creation' of wealth from finite resources. Humans can only work so long before they tire, and consumers can only buy so many of the same dress before they no longer need any more dresses. There is always a limit to the amount of money that can be made in any venture, whether it is conquest of ancient societies or mass-produced trinkets. The wells run dry, the mines empty, the storehouses fill to overflowing.

The Capitalist, like the conqueror, is never sated, since the entire point of both Capitalism and conquest is to gain ever-increasing amounts of wealth (unlike for the worker or the slave, which is do do as little work as possible while still surviving or not getting beaten). So Capitalism must find new markets, new fields of conquest from which wealth can be derived. And sometimes, it does so by destroying what is already there in order to make profit from rebuilding it.

When a neighborhood undergoes gentrification, land and buildings are changed or replaced in order derive more wealth from them. Old houses that are only being lived in or rented at stable rates become targets for Capital-seeking investors and real-estate agents. If you own a house your entire life, you're not making money for anyone else by living there. Renters provide some wealth for landlords, but because there's only so much that can be squeezed from a renter's income before they must move, Capitalists actively displace renters in favor of higher-income people.

Old houses are torn down to make room for denser apartments and condominiums, old apartments are renovated or sold as condominiums, and the people who lived there previously are either priced out or forced to leave through lease terminations.

This cycle of upheaval is not new.

Consider some of the earliest upheavals caused by Capitalism, not in the Americas or in Africa, but on the very islands where Capitalism started. The Highland Clearances and other Enclosure movements were the first salvos in the transition from Primitive Accumulation to Capitalist exploitation of peoples.

Wealthy landlords and tribal chieftains pushed people (often kin) from land they'd worked for centuries in order to derive more wealth from that land through "improvements" (in essence, the beginning of industrialised farming). Some were sold as indentured servants because of unpaid rents, others were marched away and left to die, and the vast majority faced a choice: move to the towns and work in the factories other Capitalists had set up to turn their lifeblood into wealth, or travel across oceans to the conquered lands of North America and Australia in order to start again.

Of course, the lands those displaced peoples moved to were already inhabited, and the history of all European colonies is written in the blood of indigenous peoples. Those First Nations and Aboriginal peoples had varying responses to these newcomers. Some sought peace, others sought war, but neither tactic proved successful in keeping their own ancestral lands from the Enclosures that sprung from the British Isles.

The United States, particularly, has seen multiple waves of displaced peoples. Enslaved peoples from the African continent, indentured servants and refugees from the "Progress" of Capitalism in Europe, and of course, the very people who lived on this land before the whole cycle began—they are all victims.

'Round the Prickly Pear

Gentrification is seen by many as a natural process. In a way, it is: it's initiated by a very small but particularly destructive element of the natural world—humans, or more specifically, Capitalist humans. And though displacement of peoples is not new, the kinds of economic displacement seen since the birth of Capital are a different thing altogether than what was seen in the past.

Gentrification is a kind of opening of a new Capital-producing market, created by destroying what was already there—and it's a super-heated engine of destruction in many cities of the United States currently. I've many friends in the Bay Area, for instance, for whom the exorbitant rent-increases has become so absurd that they've taken on a sort of war-trauma. The same occurs in Seattle now, with apartments friends rented 4 years ago at $1000/month now renting for $2000, a 100 increase over half-a-decade.

Similar in Portland, Oregon, as well as neighborhoods in large cities across the country. In other cities, natural disaster (like in New Orleans) or economic collapse (Detroit) have led to even more damage to Black folk, as investors and traitorous politicians have colluded to rebuild cities without their traditional inhabitants. In all cases, though, the mechanism is the same, and the victims have much more in common with each other than they do with new residents moving into their respective cities, yet rarely do they fight in solidarity.

But why not? Some of this absence of solidarity derives from racism, but there's an understated problem in our understanding of Gentrification which also prevents united fronts against Capitalist displacement.

Too much written about this process situates it in a narrative of cycles, a progression of neighborhoods derived from natural law and inevitability. From this view, the answer to complaints about rising rents and destroyed communities range between "get over it" or "there's nothing that can be done." A less-heard point sometimes arises, though, and it has more merit. I heard it often from my anarchist friends in the middle of the last decade, an important reminder that whites did this to First Nations peoples before, and we're all on stolen land.

This is true. Unfortunately, the result of that argument is usually a complete dismissal of the very real damage done to people when their homes are taken through predatory loans or their rents increased so much they have no choice to become displaced.

A Kindness of Ravens

The problem arises because so many different peoples, of different racial and ethnic backgrounds, have all fallen victim to Capitalist displacement. The land I currently live on was stolen from the Duwamish peoples more than a century ago; it is still stolen from them, and worse—the Federal Government does not recognize them as a tribal group, and therefore all their claims are legally null. The Black families who lived here were descendents of people displaced by force from their homes in Africa, victims of Primitive Accumulation and the European thirst for Capital.

And then...there's me. Some of my ancestors were displaced from the British Isles during the Enclosures and the birth of Capital. Others fled mainland Europe during the Enclosure of their land, or became refugees of Capitalist wars. Not all, mind. I've a rumored but unverified First Nations ancestor on one side of my family, and on the other, an unfortunate "Boston Brahmin" ancestor. And I've already been displaced several times in my life through poverty or rent-increases.

We could construct a hierarchy of victimhood in the relentless history of displacement by employing metrics of innocence, complicity, and ancestral ties. And we should and must tell those stories, and we should and must do everything to right those wrongs.

But here's the problem: the insidious trick of Capitalism is that the violence it perpetrates upon people determines their future actions, too. White (a false racial construction) settlers, displaced from a myriad of European lands, helped displace (sometimes by direct violence) indigenous peoples and each other, like abused children who grow up to repeat their childhood trauma upon others. The violence enacted on them became the violence they enacted upon others.

More horrifically, Capitalism offers a path out of poverty and ancestral trauma if one agrees to renounce all kin, class, and ancestral ties. The descendent of African slaves who becomes an immigration enforcement officer, the victim of the Enclosures and the Clearances who agreed to help the English enforce its laws against the Irish or became a colonial administrator in India, the Irish descendents who swelled the ranks of violent police forces in New York, Boston, and San Franscisco, the "Buffalo Soldier," the Tribal leader who signed away mining rights for personal benefit, the poor-born of any race who becomes a manager or foreman—each is preyed upon twice-over by Capitalism, forced into horrible circumstance and then offered a treasonous path to personal survival.

When we try to parse out all the histories of complicity, we miss the point, much like sorting buckets of bailed water on a sinking ship according to half-full/half-empty dichotomies. The question should not be, "who suffered most?" but rather "why haven't we stopped this suffering?"

In a gentrifying neighborhood, newcomers are often confused by the reactions of those their presence is displacing. No one person displaced another; in San Franscisco and Seattle and in all these other cities, each person is making an individual choice to live in a different place, often times following work. The problem is never each individual person, but the systematic weakening of the communities being displaced (long before real estate agents and property owners identified the neighborhood as a new market), a state which not only enables but often encourages the destruction of older neighborhoods, and under all of this, entire societies which have lost touch with the spirit of the land beneath their feet and the meaning of place.

And it's that weakening of ties to place where our primary resistance and revolutionary assault against Capitalism must begin.

From Strong Roots, We Fight

Capital requires new markets to expand, but the earth is limited and we only need so much shit. Enclosures are an old trick, and the displacement they cause not only generate both more profit for the rich, but do something even more vital for the smooth running of Capital: displaced peoples lack community, become desperate, and most significantly of all, have no access to their history.

Slaves hauled across oceans cannot visit the graves of their ancestors; peasants forced off land cannot visit the old wells and stones which rooted their world firmly in the Other. Old contracts with the land are broken, old gods forgotten, and the standards once used to judge if an act would serve the community or damage it fall away.

Capitalist displacement is also Capitalist disenchantment; it is the reason for which the traditions of people are perpetually destroyed. Rootless people are easily controlled and coerced, people without the stories, myths, and spirits of a place have nowhere to turn beside the market for the creation of their meaning.

Capitalism needs us to be displaced, pushed around by its invisible hand. We must stand and fight, root ourselves in place, learn the names of our neighbors and the trees on our streets, seek out the sources of our water, trace our streams under pavement, learn the origins of our food and the histories of our homes.

A Kindness of Ravens

We must tell the stories of our place to each other, creating new communities, new peoples unwilling to move when they tell us to go, untempted by profit in other towns, unafraid to confront the haunting ghosts of those buried in our graveyards, uncowed by threats of property laws and poverty, outside the logic of the time-sheet and the work-day.

For those of us in the Americas or in other former colonies of the proto-capitalist empires in Europe, we must begin by seeking out, offering our aid, and helping to restore the peoples displaced by our ancestral traumas. The Duwamish are not the only First Nations people written out of existence in the United States, and the successor states of British Imperialism have a particularly horrible history of violence against the people they conquered—the British, after all, started Capitalism.

We must become rooted in the land and communities, and we must refuse the Capitalist's game of divide-and-conquer. In cities like Seattle and San Francisco, waves of 'tech workers' are displacing others. They, moving to cities for high-waged work, have no ties to the land, and no community when arriving except their (Capitalist) employer and others working for them. The 100-year old Black woman whose house they might purchase means nothing to them; they don't know her story any more than they know that of the land upon which her home was built.

But we must remember—they are mere tools, buying in to new capitalist ventures and selling their labor to powerful Capitalists. They contribute to the destruction of communities by renting and buying homes at exorbitant rates (against their own self-interest). They become the weapons Capitalists wield in new wars of accumulation, often unwitting and too-often indifferent, rootless themselves, colonial settlers no different than those who became colonial servants in India for the British crown. They are not the direct cause of gentrification, but they become "class traitors," slobbering on their knees and choking at the altars of Capital—just like the rest of us. They, and we, must refuse to destroy the lives of others in return for scraps from the tables of the rich.

And from our position of rootedness and solidarity, we must directly attack Capital. It is the Capitalists who are in power, who start this engine and keep it stoked hot, making a killing from our attempts to make a living. Aided by complicit governments bloated and drunk on tax money, political donations, and their lust for power, the Capitalists have perfected the pillaging wars of Colonialism in a system so pristine we cannot fully unravel its knotted patterns of destruction.

But that knot cannot be unraveled; it must be cut. We cannot ever hope to find an answer to capitalist displacement of peoples without fighting Capitalism, nor can we hope to rectify the wrongs that Capitalism has caused to peoples until Capitalism is no longer a threat.

The answer's under our feet, in the places we live, the communities from which we're alienated, in the spirits of the air and tree and grass in our neighborhoods.

The answer is both a change of place consciousness and a resurrection of class-consciousness, a solidarity between peoples and the spirits of place, a new treaty with the land and its inhabitants (living and dead, seen and unseen). Even when displaced (as I was), we must see every place as our home and a site of beautiful resistance. And those who refused to leave, those who, like my transfer-trading friend and neighbor, who bravely choose land, history, and community over the treason of the capitalist buy-out, must be be honored, supported and defended, because it is they who can show us best the importance of roots.

We have allies, seen and unseen. We must join their fight.

The Land

Across

The Water

When I was in Wales, I dreamt of another dark bard, except I think he was also Brân. I don't know how this works, or why it's like this. Something to do with shapeshifting, I think—like the way Brân becomes the land around him when he wants your attention or is invading an island. A bit like Arianrhod inhabits the air, the shifting blue-grey-violet-rose skies while also reflecting from the surface of puddles on stone.

They wear the land around them; why not wear humans?

Except for our forgetting, except for our disenchantment, except for our separation, we are also part of the land. And therein's the gate we're looking for.

But oh, that dream was a bit torrid; so, too, what happened when I met the dragon on a hill overlooking Llyn Dinas. But what I can write about without arousal are the caverns through which I passed to meet him on the other side.

I met some druids there. One pulled my beard, hard. Wouldn't let go—I couldn't get out of his grip. He stared, I stared back. He seemed to wait for something, but I couldn't speak.

So I pulled his beard back, and he nodded and walked away. Did I mention his companion was wearing bondage gear?

Anyway, a few weeks later I'm in Chicago with a friend and we're sitting at a bar which is also "gay darkroom," and the bartender pulls my beard because he likes it, and then suddenly gets all excited (not that sort of excited) and asks if I know about the 'druid beard pullers.' I have no idea what he's talking about, but am suddenly worried because of my dream and noticing a guy walking by in bondage gear and then he looks up a picture of stone carvings depicting druids pulling each other's beards and I notice I'm underground in a basement with walls identical to those caverns and...

That's how this stuff happens.

You go a little mad at those times when past and future bend in upon the now. But that's also, usually, just the presence of a god.

Still. When they pull your beard, they mean it.

Love Notes From The Abyss, III

This prison was long ago closed, yet you broke into your cell and closed the door behind you. Good job. You've made a great slave thus far, though you've put your chains on wrong. Your manacles are loose. The noose isn't tied quite right–it's harder than you'd think to hang yourself.

We can help you with that if you really want, but you don't even know how to know what you really want.

When you ran in joy toward the light and fell, what did they tell you?
When your heart leapt in love and was broken, what did you hear?
When you tried, then failed, you listened to what they said.
"This is what you get. That's what you deserve. What did you expect? You should have known better. Have you learned your lesson?"
This is what they tell you, which is what they have been told, which is what you tell yourself, which is what you tell others.

You need no masters to enslave you. You've enslaved yourself, sitting here, all of you, arrayed in your chains, behind these bars, waiting for someone to use you. And they do.

The Land Across
The Water

In the land across the water,
in the land soaked by water,
along the land pressed by water
I offered the wool to the giant,
the wool also to The Mothers.

You're here, aren't you?

Now, the song swells, the singers first awkward, learning the words as they sing them,
The drum first unmatched rhythm 'till the rest of us catch the thread.
My arms become other arms, and I stare at them, remembering:

I'm remembering another's arms, not his, not mine, but hers, a sister-soul's arms. Neither dark nor light, not very strong, flabby, she thinks, not strong like theirs. And the other women are speaking to her, not worried that she doesn't think her arms are like theirs, knowing someone will remind her.

And I see her. And I remind her, I not her, but I also her, some fragment
of her

seeing through her eyes,
seeing what she sees,
staring in shame at her weak arms.

"They are not weak," I will at her, remembering another woman I'd seen,
strong and fierce and fat,
full of magic,
full of strength
the same color of skin,
unafraid.
"They are like hers," I try to show her, "and they are like mine."

I'm sure she saw,
I'm sure she understood.
I'm remembering her arms, and the other woman's arms, and I'm looking
at mine,
stronger than I could ever believe,
and stronger still,
because they're not just mine.

You're here, aren't you?
Like that time in the land across the waters, soaked in water,
lighting a candle to a dragon,
an offering to a giant
to be spun by the Mothers.
And maybe he shouldn't be here, but she-and-they know I can't be here
without him.
They know I come with another,
I met them with another,
that time before I traveled to the land across the water.
It'd been another him,
not this him,
though it'd been him who taught me
how to find this him,
that time they rewove my world.

The Land Across The Water

I feel him in my arms, testing them. That's how I know, and the breath at my neck,
wind from a mountain and a forest as the song arises,
the crowd weaves it together.

And there's that moment even he is a bit cynical,
florescent light and carpet and a kiddie pool;
not that they may not come,
but that we may not see.

This isn't the land across the waters, even as the bridge is lain across them.

It was another I was with last time, under pine.
Prepared the tree for weeks, waiting for when he'd arrived to introduce me,
when he told me to shut up.

The same who'd helped me meet him,
brought me down through caverns I'd later travel for
the one who'd been waiting on the other side.
Under pine, and he told me to shut up. I talk too much sometimes, huh?
He told me like a father, or a brother, both knowing me well
that I'd fill the awkward silence of their presence
with words to stave off decision.

"Shut up, give attention–they are greater than I."
And so I listened, and they laughed and cackled and jeered,
kind and harsh and indifferent,
demanding blood,
blood I couldn't draw,
blood they probably didn't want,
but blood I probably owed.
And then the mosquito bit, and then I laughed,
remembering what I'd teach myself later to do.

But this isn't the land across the water, only a bridge from here to there.
And there's awful carpet and florescence and a kiddie pool, but I'm crying anyway because it's her-and-them again,
not at a well by a great pine, but in a room above a well of the earth

where pillar and root shook and broke open and will soon again.
I'm crying because it's also him again, as he said it would be.

It's uncouth, probably, to have him here, but he can't come in anyway,
no house big enough to hold him,
not unless I bring him,
not unless he comes.
Lured to the land across the water
where waited a house big enough,
filled with knives, like the house big enough,
iron circled by flame.
You're here again.
Like a lover, I guess, you don't need say 'yes' each time he comes,
not when you give him your arms for a little while to use,
even if they are bound for a little while to his will, not yours.
Sometimes, you want to be disarmed.
And (not) my hands attached to (not) my arms caress my face as I cry, remembering them,
Just as later, there's another, like him but human, bearing banners of all my
wars,
doing the same thing, laughing at my groaning sighs, delighting in my
heaving growls.

"Be ready," he said. "A god bit the cup you offered."
But before that dream,
the banners tattered,
she-and-they stand in a well as I cry as he
runs (not) my fingers through (not) my beard.
And I lean into him,
him leaning into me, and neither of us are there
and both are there as
she-and-they stand in that well.

I remember–I stood upon that bridge and listened.
I remember—I walked along that fence and gathered.

The Land Across The Water

I remember, I sat under that tree and bled.
I remember–he told me what would come.

Mothers of victory, Matrona. Mothers of the tribes Matrona.
I'm crying, and he's there,
and she-and-they are there,
and there's the copper in the hand and the wish uttered,
what he would ask of them for me, what I would ask of them with him,
and we walk together.
He's heavy, there at the back,
there at the side, leaning in,
leaning through, and we kneel together,
the coin in the pool, Matrona, the Mothers.
And then the banners after the river-forded,
alder-pilings trampled,
strong and creaking across the river,
the bridge held over the cracking fault
beneath the land where water springs through,
the dead gather along the lake,
the ancient forests climb older mountains to watch.
A god bit the cup he was offered, pleased, as other gods nod, as the
Mothers laugh, smiling, as he runs hands (his)(mine) through my beard
and crows call to wake us both
both into
the land across the water.

A Marshland Hearth (Travel Journals, I)

8 December: What You Can Tell a Forest

I'll start with the last few days. Or should I start with the last few weeks? Or months? I don't know. Everything runs together. Time folds in on itself, ties itself into knots which meet and bind past events into the present, strands of the future somewhere there in bound echoes about to return.

Here is the sea. Here is not the sea. Here is a swamp, waiting for the sea, biding years until the waters rise and it returns to what we all want to be again before returning to the stars.

I'm at a table staring out a darkening window past a window into false light.

I'm here again.

Here is a table in a house of my sister in the dredged and managed swamplands of central Florida, marsh which despite all the efforts of humanity continues, sodden, in the foreign-yet familiar mists falling from the very close sky.

Asphalt and concrete flatten the land, but unlike the streets and highways of Seattle, they seem more like tenuous and temporary tracks across wet sand and thick-bladed grass. Retention ponds and canals do their best to direct the ancient floods, but they seem mere puddles and ditches, not hewn but dug like the small channels a child's hand might make on the shore for crashing waves to follow.

I'm here again.

"Here" is my sister's home, where

"sage-blue tufts drape over branches, gossamer ribbons adorning the shade-queen of the summerlands. Willow mourns, but at night, so too does Oak, a dirging dance of stillness, unnoticed steps through silver light seeping through clouded skies."

I remember when I wrote that, where I sat, what I thought. Words scattered but inscribed become sigils and glyphs holding fragments of myself to be unlocked, invoked, call forth and scattered again upon winds carrying rains back to the sea.

I remember having no idea, being guided by someone else who is apparently me, me later, me when I know what I'm doing telling myself when I've no fucking clue which thing before me must be done, what fragment of unheard music must be strained towards, which words come next after the ones just written.

Others help. Gods dancing in mists and mountains and bigger by far, great forces to which we've given names they revealed.

They help, like an earthquake helps settle the land, revitalize the city.

They help, like volcanoes help grow our crops and strengthen the forests.

They help, like hurricanes sow seeds and water the fields.

So many warnings not to ask them for help, and I smile at my foolishness.

Others help, and are myriad. Land spirits are like lovers, so many gifts, so many obligations in any relationship.

The night before I left I missed a bus, another was late. I'd called upon a lover, she-he of the pool, who demanded I call upon my lover, they of the trees. Only someone like me doesn't pack until midnight before leaving for four weeks, only someone like me ignores the demand because he's afraid to say good-bye.

I'd written about her-him, so many blues of grey, and she-he's standing there holding a circlet of light when I arrive, a parting gift I almost scorned because I didn't want to say good-bye.

Before her-him, the tree I'd blessed, its roots uprooting the sidewalk, the notice posted a warning. Didn't know 80 year-olds had monetary value, a 10 grand/mother Maple who "might" be removed. Water from elsewhere, a call to others, a blessing and hope that she'd survive the concrete replacement.

Why should a tree have to survive replacement of cement and gravel?

But she did, the gorgeous hobbled lady, branches so absurdly clipped and shaped by men's insistence that she do what they say they grew outward, away and around the lines strung through her, ever outward from the center of her shapely trunk that maybe no one noticed had become a great wheeled crown.

But my last good-bye had to wait for sleep, all two hours of it before I trudged down a hill with rucksack and pack to the entrance. Sunrise exploding crimson against dawning, tired clouds, and I at the tree-line.

There wasn't enough time to sit on the bridge, or to light the candle in the hollowed stump by the elk-tooth. Only a brief "I love you," sudden sobs, and a muttered, "this is scary, you know."

Because you can tell forests things like that.

These forests here you can tell other things, the things you say to people you don't need to be brave for, to people you don't need to console or counsel, to lovers who have no needs and friends who've seen so much light your darkness is but welcome, cooling shade.

Your words wash through them like the rain, so many ponds and streams rinsing sepia tannins from sandy soil, water clear and warm and sometimes full of sulphur in the few places the water wells up.

9 December: They Watch Our Fire, From Forests

Here, we are then. Here, we are before the fire, flames licking the flesh of trees as Her moon rises with Her stars, I with my words and you with yours.

I am best by a fire.

A candle sits on stones raised upon the flame, dedicated to the Lady of the Flame, and I sit before it, writing you, but really writing me. I'm always writing to myself, because I am always forgetting, always astonished at the remembering. I felt like that, I remind myself, from earlier to later, just as I guide myself from now to before.

To write is to slip out of time, sit before a fire with a candle, sipping tea after beer, distant white lights suspended from a moon-lightened sky, his face still in your vision, his words warm as the fire, knowing you've slipped outside time.

Like a reflection in a mirror regarded, and the mirror is gone. Like words on a screen read, and the screen is ignored. Stare at the glass, at the thin back-lit frame, and you've slipped outside of time, or back into it, depending only on your thoughts at the time.

The sun drenched the world when I woke today, like the rains drenched the world yesterday.

I'm so exhausted.

Before I left was the book, the review, the essays. Calming the mad replying to voices that sometimes I'd see: the "special friend who stands over there in the light every night" according to the client who's words I've no reason to doubt. The rush to prepare the forest for the coming snows, the hours over the hearth melting wax for candles. Tea with friends and their children, coffee which stretched for hours, watching leather-daddy friends don rubber uniforms while prescribing my "thinking" Paganism a long "bulldog fuck."

Sure, it's true–I think too much, but do I need to make sense here?

My life there in Seattle makes little sense; any raid on the inarticulate diminishes the experience. I could say plainly "I was busy restoring a forest, making candles, meeting friends and working." But that's not my life. No one reads a book where someone goes to work and comes home, and unfelt anecdotes make poor stories:

The moon's up.

Or:

Above me hangs the moon.

Or:

Gossamer threads of moonlight glisten silver upon the waxed surface of unfamiliar leaves of Southern oak, shattering and shimmering ghostly filaments in the light midnight breeze as smoke curls from embers and licking flames, rising to meet the play of shadowed life.

Who could live otherwise?

Today I woke into sunlight after the mists of yesterday, the marsh-air chill and clear, that electric sense in the breath that warns life will soon be different. Berlin, too, is built upon a swamp, and the air there keeps you awake all night, full of life inhabited by spirits.

I read of Berlin to a forest-faced friend as we sat by this fire, because he's the sort of person who should go there, because he's the sort of person to whom one wants to read.

A Kindness of Ravens

Also, Berlin is in my head and will not leave. I was last here after my last pilgrimage; I am here again before my next. I don't know Dublin, nor Caernarfon. I would not have known to choose these places, had they not been chosen for me.

I would not have chosen much of any of this, had it been only my choice. You can't know how beautiful something will be until you've gotten there, how beautiful someone will be until you've known them. This thing about "free-will" has always been a joke, because the moment you've chosen, you must give up all choice. We only have short moments in crossroads, at the still-points of the world before entering back into time, which is also out of time.

What has become of me?

Last year I arrived here from old stones, giants muttering in my sleep, wild boars rummaging my affects, old notes echoing back into new songs, mountains with forgotten temples trying to get me to remember.

And I ask why I should remember. I am no one, when I am at my best, which is just before I am also at my worst.

When the sun set here I saw again her stars and trembled at the memory, trembled at what I've been letting myself pretend I'm not forgetting.

There's a life that threads itself out of the tapestry we thought we're weaving. We're never the only ones at the loom.

These are the thoughts you have before a fire, the same firepit into which you offered three year's of words, tearing each page from a book as you read them, laughing with laughter that wasn't your own. Brighid wanted "important paper," and it was the most important all.

Certain words only become spells when committed to flames. "Something's coming," I'd written, "or Someone" on the last page of that journal, the last entry before the fires came, before I noticed I'd entered a forge.

I'm in marshlands before a hearth-fire under a familiar moon, surrounded by spirits of memory, the few spirits I'm ever certain are actually mostly "in my head."

But a land is a relationship, land spirits are warm friends. It's not lost on me how the moon's the same as when I saw her with him. She remembers like I do, I suspect, remembers the welling hope and awkward fumbling under the moon, almost the same time last year. Like friends return bits of yourself after the distance of years, love never lost to the heart, perhaps she remembers, too, offering back to me what she gathered, what we left.

I'd fallen awfully hard for him, a most delightful soul. Like me, a being not quite in-place with where he lives, not quite in-time with his age. Filmmaker, satyr, bleeding thoughts through his words that aren't quite ready to survive this world until it's changed to greet him.

Awkward fumbling on a stone under those branches, passion locked in movements not quite in time with music neither of us could hear. And he, later, his face like a forest, said "You deserve someone to ravenously explore your castle." And he, adding, said "I'm not very hungry at the moment."

Everyone should be let down so exquisitely.

Share dreams with someone and you slip out of time, or your dreams escape into the world between the walls, waiting. It takes little for their return, waiting, suspended, a stash of hope, a forgotten cache of joy, never lost, only displaced.

And the land knows best where it's hidden, because these sometimes are our unbidden gifts to them.

By this fire, sharing my brother-in-law's ale, sharing our new lack of fear as the spirits watch, quietly, dancing to our words. I've only now just realized they were there as I write these words.

What else watches our love, laughing? Who else peers through moon-silver branch as we speak, or kiss, or sigh?

10 December: Summerlands Waiting For The Sea

The air today longs, languid memories hanging in the air like summer motes of pollen in sepia-stained even-ing.

But the days are short, shorter than those days suspended in memory of endless summer. The shortest soon arrives, and I'll greet it in a tomb.

I'm not ready. I'm not ever ready. You don't leave a place when you've prepared, else you never leave. You do not summon love, it arrives upon you and you could not have known. Death does not come when things are all gotten into order and tidy, it comes only when it's time.

And on time, I've still slipped out of it. Not that strange stroke of misfortune where every hour is wrong, events pass and you were not there. That other time, that time out-of-time, when mysteries walk with you and trees dance with volition.

A Kindness of Ravens

Everything breathes, but only out-of-time can we feel their exhalations and not suffocate.

I leave here tomorrow, having only just arrived.

This stop before Ireland was the original plan before all those other events conspired to send me across an ocean, a summons it seemed foolish to leave unanswered.

I lived much of my adolescence in the dredged southern marshes, struggling to be something unknown and unimagined by the asphalt and beaches, the shopping centers and suburbs. I fled the swamps, first to the old brick of New England, then to the old trees of the Northwest, skirting the borders between temperate and boreal, in search of chill mists where dreams of the Other hide in fern and cloud.

Last year, I finally returned, after a decade away, long enough time between what I'm always becoming and what is only offered that I would no longer sink in these swamps.

Months with family I'd too-little seen, the warmest of hearths, food and drink and dancing life.

It's here, last year, I began writing things other people wanted to read. It was here, last year, I decided what I wanted to become. Enough time away, enough time being other, enough time in the Other and any land seems to rise to greet you, offering strange gifts to your own fumbled giftings.

The land makes you, as we make everything from the land.

What I am and think and feel in Seattle is not what I am and think and feel here. Re-reading my words, I note the subtle qualities of the in-breathed air in the sentences I form.

Seattle is all edge, uneven land surrounded by water, floating above a fault. To rest there is to stare into distraction, to quiet the unheard noise of welling fire and crushing rocks beneath your feet.

Here is waiting for the sea, basking in light even in the chilling winter, greens and blues making violet somehow in the shadows, vibrant scent of fecund evening lingering long into night. I dream of the summerlands, visions dancing just-out-of-sight of ancient life painted with even older art.

Tomorrow, a plane, an ocean. The dreams will fade, become other dreams I've never seen. Leaving the warm hearth of family will not be easy, and I shall miss the languid longing breaths of the spirits of these silent, watching trees.

In The Time of The Dead
(Travel Journals, II)

There was a time before clocks.

Not a time before time, of course. There's always been time, marked by events common to most of us foolish beasts cursed with self-referential sentience. The sun rises, it is morning. It sets, it's evening. There was the dark part of the day and light part of the day, the middling of both. Moon rises in his-her varying shades and patterns cycled the month for us, storms and heat and snow, falling and budding of leaf, pregnant vine and heavy branch, birthing of animals and melting of ice all told to us the time.

The time after clocks is ferocious, brutal, insistent. At 2:30 pm I leave for work, and if I have left at 2:45pm I will not be there "on time." A friend to meet at noon, because if not-noon she cannot meet, a date to end by 11 lest he not ever catch his bus home to be in bed by midnight so to work by 9.

Astronomical events no longer trigger and compel and direct activity; ciphers do, numbers mis-representing themselves as important.

But I've slipped out of time.

11-12 December:...A Different, Inaccurate Map

It was much harder to leave the marshlands than I'd expected. A short trip, a few days' visit before heading off to Ireland—I'd known it'd be brief, quite temporary, but I hadn't been prepared for how strongly the land there would call back to me. Or, rather, how strongly I'd find myself listening.

Stronger than that, however, was being in such a warm, settled, kind hearth.

One day perhaps I'll tell again the stories of my youth, the 13 year old me with the developmentally-disabled schizophrenic single mother and the two younger sisters, us all on our own and I the only one with enough access to the world outside to figure out how rent might be paid, food might be found, and how we'd all managed to survive the even harsher life then we'd left in Appalachia.

That story's for another time, really.

I'm sitting in an ancient stone building on the coast of Wales as a storm whips outside the windows of this hotel, sipping tea at a large wooden table near a massive castle and a dream-haunting rock. It's time for other stories, first

One has to have a sense of time to travel, of course, particularly now in our grand time-regulated modern present. A plane from Orlando to Dublin leaves at 8:05pm, the gates for it close at 7:45pm. To arrive at 7:50pm is to not go to Dublin.

And that's all "Eastern Standard Time," of course. Back in the Northland forests, the time is different. In Dublin, the time is different. Here in Wales I write at 1am, but you in the vast urban stretches of New York are not yet preparing for bed, and you in cities-on-the-bays of Northern California are just now noting the end of daylight.

The time of plane travel is particularly brutal, as are the places you meet those planes. Ursula K. Le Guin has already described airports quite better than I ought try. From *Changing Planes*, an absurdly fantastic little book:

> *"In the airport, luggage-laden people rush hither and yon through endless corridors, like souls to each of whom the devil has furnished a different, inaccurate map of the escape route from hell."*

Vast complexes all regulated by time (and fear), areas you cannot go, things you cannot do, all so to get into long metal boxes full of others as miserable as you are, cramped into tiny and unpleasant seats where you are woken every 20 minutes by offers of soda or shopping opportunities.

And beyond the airports are the airplanes, where you are not only already engaging in body-stressing high-speed travel, you're also transgressing time, passing the artificial markers humans have overlaid upon our geographies to arrive hours before you started, or many more hours later than you traveled.

And so it was as such I woke in a plane landing in Dublin, the day already broken across unfamiliar skies. Uncomfortable, dehydrated, constipated and irradiated people scrambled over each other to retrieve belongings from tiny cabinets above what we politely refer to as "seats" within our great modern accomplishment, all to wait another interminable length of time to exit the plane, retrieve more belongings, and shuffle, sore, through customs lines.

I should maybe here admit I do not like customs, or immigration, or body scanners and checkpoints. I am always a little surprised when I am distractedly waved through Homeland Security, discovering each time to both my delight and disappointment I've not yet done anything important enough to be considered a risk to aviation. I suspect they're all quite aware that I'm quite cowed by the entire process and consider aviation more of a risk to my soul.

And though I get along quite well with most police folks, seem to pass by most of their notice and avoid their attention, I always tremble before the confessional box of Customs and Immigrations.

And security at Dublin? It's brutal, as my experience should show.

I stood, exhausted, sore, cramped and fogged before the great gate and handed over my passport. The immigration official opened its crumpled and dog-eared pages and shook his head before turning his gaze towards me and saying, "Ye' seem the nice sort, yeah? Easy-going an' all that?"

"I think so?" I answered. "I mean, I think I am?"

I stood there, suddenly overcome with self-doubt. Am I really the nice sort? I'm mostly nice, usually polite. Sometimes not as nice as I could be. Sometimes awfully brusque if I haven't had my tea yet.

And easy going? Fuck—sometimes I'm a bit of a humorless old man. I never get other people's sarcasm, often times get a bit stressed when I'm responsible for things and they're not going quite right, I'm…

I looked back at the guy behind the visa window, wondering if he could sense all this. This was certainly his plan: trigger an existential crisis in a potential terrorist until they confess all those times they've never been quite as easy-going about the world as they could be, how sometimes they've really not been very nice at all.

And then there's another immigration enforcer, a burly, stern man standing next to him, and they're talking, and I'm not looking forward to an Irish holding cell and a forced return to America where I'll only get more of this sort of treatment, where I'll definitely not be known as being "the nice sort" or even slightly "easy going."

A Kindness of Ravens

The two men staring at my passport shook their heads. The first flipped through each wrinkled page while the other observed, his visage one of paternalistic disdain.

And finally they speak, words I'd been dreading:

"I wish I had an iron."

"An iron?" I ask, utterly confused by this terrifying Kafka-esque turn.

Neither of them answer my question as they inexplicably return my passport. "Have fun," says the first, and I'm really confused.

"Is...is that all I need?"

He nodded, and I shuffled away, staring at my passport, noting finally that he'd been uncreasing the dog-ear edges of its pages for me.

And then I was out, out into Dublin or, more specifically, outside the airport in Dublin, smoking my first cigarette in 12 hours and wondering why the rest of the world isn't so nice as Irish customs officials.

12-13 December: City of the Dead

Slipping out of time while traveling is great for hearing things you don't normally hear. Out of the familiarity of the normal and habitual, senses which fall into disuse and atrophy re-awaken jarringly, as if grumpy and rather pissed they've been disturbed.

Suddenly alert for everything because you don't quite know what you can ignore, every noise, every voice, every distant sound presents itself urgently, overwhelming the usual manner of sorting such sounds.

You're deafened, and a bit blinded, and a bit numbed from so much.

Like the blind, you can rely on what you know of other things to make guesses regarding what's in front of you. Just as the feel of one door teaches you most of what you need to know about most doors, the distancing on one staircase gives you a framework to understand other stairs, some cities teach you the most important things about other cities like it.

A European city teaches quite a bit about other European cities. Paris and Berlin are radically different, yet knowing one can guide you into knowing the other or another of its kind. American cities, however, are useless for imparting any such knowledge about how to get around a European city, but the largest European ones make using the New York City subway system seem like child's play.

Dublin, then, is like Paris, or Berlin, but with many more dead. In Dublin the dead are roaming about unhindered and unguided—you hear them along with all the city sounds, all the traffic sounds and people sounds and dog barking sounds—all the living sounds and then the dead sounds.

Dublin is a city of the dead.

You know? I'm embarrassed a bit of how little Irish history I'd remembered, how little of the last 300 years of the place I'd recollected. I can tell you what happened in Bretagne, or Wales, but Ireland? I'd forgotten too much of it.

But then I began to remember, because it's all in front of you, all the dead. You pass by a field and ask your companion what's there and he says the answer you're trying not to listen to: the dead. Lots of them, all buried together in a mass grave, the "Croppies Acre" of Republican rebels at the turn of the 19th century. Signs directing you to tombs of fallen revolutionaries are everywhere. But you don't really need the signs, because they're roaming the sea-tinged air as you walk through the streets, trying to get your attention

And trying to get my attention.

I remember when I didn't listen to the dead, didn't note their strange hollow pre-electric voices and whispers, heard best not in graveyards but in taverns, not best on Samhain but on Beltaine, not during the times where we go looking for them but in those hours and in those places where they come looking for us.

I don't quite know what else to say about this. I should probably conceal these words in poetic musings for those who don't hear the dead, or don't think such a thing is likely or even possible. Poets have done this for centuries, speaking on the fallen with such metaphor anyone might merely encounter such recollections as mere muse-struck rantings.

I could say, perhaps, how the air seems haunted or fragmented echoes of their lives return or some other thing, and leave it at that.

But no. Dublin is a city of the dead. They're fucking everywhere, gating through the very stones, lending a chthonic strength to an other, peculiar thing you note upon treading the streets of this city:

The city's smeared with anarchist and revolutionary propaganda.

A few days before I arrived, there'd been a large anti-government rally around attempts to begin charging individuals for water use. Because of years of government neglect of public infrastructure during the Neo-Liberal policies of the first decade this millennium, Dublin's water distribution is failing.

A Kindness of Ravens

In case you don't remember or never heard, Ireland was called "the Celtic Tiger" because of its willingness to accept international investments without taxing the corporations who benefited from the government's welcome. Its economy suddenly appeared to be booming as more and more foreign companies set up there to take advantage of low corporate tax rates, while the government did what every other government's done in such situations–stopped spending on infrastructure.

The perennial promise of jobs has tricked many a people into opening themselves to pillaging, just as sometimes the promise of a promotion or true love promises many into giving over their bodies to a ravaging, but of any people, the Irish have been ravaged and pillaged more than most.

Now private companies have begun to install water meters into homes in Dublin so the government may begin charging for usage, despite the fact that its citizens already pay for water through a water-tax.

Thousands of people gathered in defiance, blockading the entrances to neighborhoods where the meters were to be installed, and they were visited by a special delegation of people who've fought the same war in their own city–Detroit. The Detroit Water Brigade was here, standing both in solidarity and alliance to the resistance against water privatization and government negligence of the most basic of things governments claim to provide their people. What use is a government, really, if it does not ensure the water keeps running?

Those familiar with The Morrígan and the questions of sovereignty may already understand this matter, first brought to my attention by Judith O'Grady's *God-Speaking*. Rulers have always been expected to ensure the right-running of a society's basic needs. When the crops fail or enemies invade, the governed blame (rightly or wrongly) their rulers, as true in ancient Ireland or Greece as it is now in modern France or Canada. When rulers fail to protect the people they rule, it is, even in modern society, seen as sort of message from the gods that the ruler is no longer fit to rule. Presidents who preside over great economic suffering are voted out, Kings and even Dictators in such circumstances are deposed.

Here, then, in Dublin begins one of those crises. The water system is failing, some communities must boil their water. The government proposes to fix this not with the money they've already collected, but by collecting more money through private means.

And the city resists, and the dead resist with them.

One doesn't need study too deeply to see what the dead have seen, how the people have always been fucked, be it by foreign powers or by their own governments. The dead remember, and in Dublin, the dead do not stay still.

The dead have slipped out of time.

To be out of time is not to forget.

The past and the present are not so far apart, they are mere neighbors in the same country of memory, adjacent hillsides or mountains comprising a ridge or a range, trees next to each other becoming a grove or a forest.

The dead do not forget because they are in the place of all remembering, waiting only for the living to remember them.

14. December: Running To The Sea

I woke at 4am on Sunday morning, after a full day traveling with my host, a day which ended with a sudden, minor panic.

I was due to take a ferry across the Irish Sea to Wales to meet my best friend, and because I've had so little sleep these last few days, I waited a little too long to purchase my ferry ticket. All afternoon sailings were booked, leaving me only the option of 8am or 10pm, and only the early sailing would allow me to arrive in time to take a train to my next stop, Caernarfon.

I may have slipped out of time, but the rest of the world has not.

I noticed my mistake at 11pm on Saturday night and purchased the early ticket. 8am isn't bad in most places, but 8am on a Sunday morning in a heavily Catholic country might as well be 4am—there were no buses that would get me to the terminal in time.

I certainly guess I might have taken a taxi, but taxis cost money and feet are free, so, after managing to sleep a full hour (jetlag's still got me), I hefted my rucksack and set off on what became a two-and-a-half hour forced march along the Liffey to the Port three hours before sunrise.

It occurs to me one can spin such a predicament however one likes. Certainly the prospect of waking into a cold and wet and very dark city well before dawn after only one hour of sleep and trudging quickly to catch a ferry carrying 40 pounds of stuff on your back is a miserable thing, except when it's the most thrilling thing you can possibly think of.

Actually, I kinda love this sort of shit.

A Kindness of Ravens

Alone as the wind whipped past me in a city I don't know, surrounded by the voices of the dead and sleeping souls, I walked along the River Liffey and followed her dark, brooding, somber passage through the streets of Dublin, my head full of thoughts mostly my own.

The sights I saw will haunt me for ages, particularly as I drew closer to the sea. The city that was and the city that is stood together, dripping sky-tears into the river at my right as clouds hid and revealed the year's last half-moon in the final days before Midwinter.

I really didn't have the time to stop, but when I came upon a set of emaciated statues, I pretty much had no choice.

By the "International Financial District," (Dublin's occupied "Green-Zone" from the Neo-Liberal invasion), there stands a parade of statues, an understated memorial to the victims of the Irish famine.

There's something we tend to forget about famines, and particularly the Irish ones. But what the dead remember and the living mostly do not is this: the famine and mass exodus of Irish folks was caused by the failure of a crop only as much as the flooding of New Orleans was caused by a hurricane or the Dust Bowl was caused by bad weather. Potatoes aren't even native to Ireland.

Here, amongst the new foreign banks, the start-ups, the financial and tech firms all eager to bring a decidedly un-modern land into the Modern, there stands these statues. They are emptied shells, almost impossible to look at for very long, depictions of humans so desperate to survive their new starvation, a famine caused by the next new thing of their time (that is, the birth of Capitalism), and they shamble near the docks, forever frozen alongside the next new thing of our time.

The irony is almost as painful as their wretched faces in the moonlight by the river, their strained, desperate, despairing looks crying "remember."

More than anywhere, it was here I felt the dead, the dead who do not forget, as much as we the living try to forget them.

To be in time is to be separated from our memory, here in the forgetting, but it's the dead, outside of time, who remain to remind us.

Dark Night Interlude
(Travel Journals, III)

To be a pilgrim, you must crumble like a great stone tower, hewn blocks tumbled-down to build the old cottages that have ruined you.

Flesh and leaves of your soul must rot underfoot into the forests through which you travel.

You must flood into the rivers that water the lands you've traveled to visit, even as you drown under those currents.

Cast out onto the sea, you must fall with the rain and become the gales of wind which chill you.

You must be burnt to ashes in the fires of a thousand hearths, and be born into each sun's rising.

In the face of every other that you meet, you must there see your face, reflected back, and in between every you and every other is the Other.

This is also how you meet the gods.

Metaphor's End (Travel Journals, IV)

The past was all metaphor, right? Myths just ways of encoding knowledge about nature, something easy to remember and something never more than it appears to be. Let the metaphor escape its imprisonment and it'll wreak havoc on the mind, the soul, the world. It's safer without magic, and gods, the fae and the dead.

Which is why I found myself clinging to the side of a mountain to talk to a giant.

14 December: When They Pull Your Beard, They Mean It

Which story do I tell? The story inside my head, the story around me, the story of the places I've been, the story of the dead in the dream pulling my beard?

The story you need to hear, the story you want to hear, the story I want to tell you, the story I think I should tell?

There's no end to the stories already, and I've only been in Wales for four days. They're weaving, threading, pulling, carding out bits and spinning and smoking like the gleaned wool gathered off the fence and offered upon the candle in the trunk of the tree, flames of...

Sorry. I'm not there yet.

I'm here, at a table in a hotel bar, an old stone building not much older than the United States, I fear, sipping coffee (the tea's terribly weak 'round these parts) trying to figure out what I'm going to tell you about everything I've seen which is suddenly making my hands tremble as I type all of this.

I may not make sense, because I've given up on metaphor, because metaphor's exploded all around me and now none of those things you hope can hide in symbol–to stay put there in signification, tied to the safe sigils of our representations–are willing to be put back into the prisons we've made for them.

Oh, oh, I know why poets go mad.

I took a photo that I thought might help. It's just a tower and a tree on a hill overlooking the Strait of Menai across the way from the city of Caernarfon. Nothing else, no metaphor, no additional meaning except for the part where you couldn't stop looking at them from the medieval city walls and really, really had to go up there.

But oh! I haven't told you that I'm in Caernarfon yet, have I?

Sorry. I've slipped out of…oh, you know.

I boarded a ferry from Dublin to the port of Holyhead on the Isle of Anglesy. The ferry's a bit more a miniature cruise-ship than what you might consider when you think ferry, and most definitely nothing Stygian, unless Charon decided to install a theatre, cafe, Bureau d'exchange and a small convenience store to distract you from the difficulties of your passage into Hades. Oh, and wireless internet, which did not afford me the opportunity to do any writing on account of my website being blocked through the local filter for "alternative beliefs."

So I slept, and dreamt a bit until the ferry approached, anticipation jarring me awake. I was going to Wales, you see, and also Nick.

Best friends are great people and should never be gotten rid of, or forgotten, or let to roam off into foreign lands without an occasional visit or perhaps a jaunt together through the lands of your gods.

Taught me how to feed crows, and had dreams of Druid Rhyd long before I got around to even thinking about being a Druid. When you tell a stranger that his glasses make him look like a bike cop, he may punch you in the face, or may, some 12 years later, help you find Caer Arianrhod and Dinas Affaoron and nod when you mutter half-sensical things about the divine figures showing up in your dreams, and the wild colors behind your closed eyelids, and he may even give you cookies.

He moved to Wales more than a year ago; in fact, a week after I left Seattle on my last pilgrimage. And he was waiting for me at Holyhead, once an ancient Druid stronghold, now a ferry-port.

What do you really say to someone after so long when you're finally standing in front of each other? Not much, really, except "well–you're here," and, "hey. You too." 'Cause more than that's just extra words to fill a rather contented silence.

All the other words come later, mostly laughs and grunted assent when he'd hear me gasp and groan and try to hold back nauseated ecstasy staring at the countryside of Anglesy and Gwynedd. Nausea–yes, because it seemed almost my body revolted against the ancient landscape, the way you want to vomit because you're so in love or want to tear off all your flesh because it's limiting the movement of your soul, anchoring your spirit a little too heavily to all what is trying to comprehend what it's seeing.

One moment you're elsewhere and another moment you're brutally here and want to break apart, disintegrate, return into the elements from which you were hewn, become tree and grass and bacteria and star and cloud and stone again. Sentience is suddenly a prison as the streams rush past you, the gnarled trees stare back, beckoning you to join them, trees your recognize, trees what are kin.

The Alchemists called this *nigredo*, the blackening, the moment you are dis-membered, unmade. The mystics called it The Dark Night, where you are left raw, broken and unpieced just before you can be put back together. The Alchemists used alembics, the mystics prayed in cells, and both are much more preferable containers than a train compartment.

Underslept, we napped, woke, roamed the city a bit. It was all a bit much to take in too quickly, castle walls and a nearby holy mount and a gentle rain and the horrid, nagging, impossible-to-shake feeling I'd known this land before.

15 December: Standing Stones and Sheep Shit Aren't Just Symbols

I don't think I can tell you about the dreams.

I'm certain I can't describe the colors to you, because they don't exist: fierce golds hewn of green tinged with copper, violets both blue and white and crimson, browns breaking apart into all the colors which comprise them.

I'd never seen such colors, and they made it a bit hard to sleep.

Also, the voices–a myriad of them all telling me things I needed to know, or what they thought I needed to know, the dead, but a different dead, dead with faces, dead with faces I thought I recognized until I saw their faces and knew I knew them from another time-out-of-time.

I woke, exhausted, the way you wake when you've dreamt those dreams where you're elsewhere, not in bed any longer. Mostly, those dreams come and I do not remember them—but wake exhausted and know I was elsewhere and then someone mentions I was in their dreams.

This often felt a betrayal, my untethered soul roaming widely, unhappy to remain close to the body it went to bed with. I've found it much easier to laugh off a lover who's out with others as I sleep, than to find my soul's been out teaching people to do things I don't even quite know how to do yet, handing them flowers to eat or warning them about impending trials to which I myself remained utterly ignorant.

I mind a bit less, like one becomes accustomed and even warmed to a lover's night-rovings, comprehending that he brings back new patterns and ferocity he'd not have learned otherwise.

Souls and lovers go elsewhere–this must be embraced if we're to have any sanity at all about the world. It was on one of those roving nights I got my name, so I can't really complain.

Oh. That was here, or there's a gate here, anyway.

Nick and I took a bus along the coast to the wet moors where, on old British Ordnance maps and on some tourist maps is marked a sunken island, visible only at low tide, called Caer Arianrhod.

Perhaps you do not know the story, and so I will tell you the story.

A wizard-king had an odd geas put upon him: he could only rest when his feet were lain upon the lap of a maiden, lest he always be at war. One of his nephews desired the particular lap-maiden of the king and asked his brother Gwydion to help him gain her. Through trickery, she is "gotten" (actually, brutally raped), and when the king finds out, he compensates the raped woman and turns the two nephews (the rapist and the accomplice) into mated pairs of animals to "get" upon each other for three years.

But the search remained for another maiden for the king to rest his feet upon, and Gwydion, now human again, suggests his half-sister Arianrhod, who lived in a castle upon an island. When the king uses magic to verify her maidenhood, she has two children, one belonging to the sea and the other a misshapen thing which grows quickly into a man.

A Kindness of Ravens

That man was Lleu Llaw Gyffes, and Dinas Dinlle was said to be his home, an eroded hill what's left of a 2500 year old ring fort, about a third of which now taken by the sea.

To get there, you can take a road. That's the awfully easy way, and that one poet said something about how glad he was about going the way less traveled and anyway it was pretty, so we didn't take the road but instead—well.

Okay. Look. When you walk into a field with a standing stone and everything you know and hear is telling you to go up to it and see if it wouldn't mind if you pass through, don't do what we did and decide we'd be all mannish and just sort of wave hello at it while all the sheep are staring at us in amazement at our audacity.

In Bretagne a decade ago, a lover and I traipsed merrily up to a really interesting-looking standing stone and then found ourselves running in abject terror for about 20 minutes until we were fully out of its view. I should know better.

So, shin deep in mud and sheep shit and our path blocked in the most intriguingly absurd ways, barriers which seemed to spring from the earth itself and the whim of some rather put-out yet bemused community of who-knows-who, we finally admitted our mistake when about to ford a small stream. The mud went much deeper than it should have, and the plank I offered my friend to help him ford landed as far from his sinking body as possible while still managing to blind him with mud.

It was Nick who remembered the standing stone first, and as he said it we both knew what we'd gotten ourselves into, and there was nothing else to be said.

We said our apologies as sheep stared, unblinking, and returned to the road.

We stopped for coffee and tea at the foot of Dinas Dinlle and my soul started untethering. I write this all now, despite its beauty, with what I can only describe as dread. Not terror, nor fear, not even anxiety, but sacred dread, the moment you know you go to meet gods closer to where they've been known, by greater gates than the ones you've uncovered or created elsewhere.

It's one thing, I guess, to meet a god in a tiny woodland or at a shrine you've tended, a different thing altogether to go to where many others have found them. Back in Seattle, or in Eugene, or elsewhere in America I could approach them still with the veil of metaphor. No matter how real they are, relics of defensive symbolism still trigger, screening, shaping, and shading them from the full dread of their existence. You can alter a shrine, re-arrange an altar, leave a grove and pretend for a little while that you are untouched.

No matter how thoroughly I've convinced myself that they are real, I still ask myself constantly if they are, and here is Njord walking awfully close to me along the shoreline as I go to sit as close as I can in sight of Caer Arianrhod and I'm breaking into pieces even as I find a sea-soaked Alder wand wash up near a stone where I sat and fuck every metaphor I've ever held up as a shield against the Other.

You can find the sunken island without looking when you learn to give attention to those things you fear are your imagination. And you can tell yourself it's just a sunken reef and she was just a character in a Christianized story and you can try to forget everything else you're seeing as all the images flood in to drown your mind like the opened floodgates of the Isle of Ys.

Or you can just listen and let those waves wash over you, listen to what they're telling you and not fight them.

This is a good land to learn to do this.

The earth is heavy here, so green and sodden and strong. Sleep is deep here, and the throngs who speak to you as you dream may be brusque, but they're telling you something you need to know, and it's all metaphor when your soul goes roaming only because that's how you speak.

16 December: Otters Are Also a Bit Much

I can't tell you about the dream this day, except that I couldn't stop thinking about it until I finally slept again.

Know that feeling where someone who doesn't exist is making love to your soul?

And then he tells you he'll wait for you, because he knows you're on your way?

And as you go to find him, there are all these other people who know you, because they were there when you got your name because that's probably how they all got their names too, and the markings on their faces tell you more than you remember to know about them?

And the man who pulls your beard and so you pull his harder because you know what he's on about and is speaking without speaking, telling you who you're gonna have to hang off a cliff-face to talk to?

And you wake and you've almost had too much, so you go take photos of trees and towers and watch an otter with your best friend because, fuck, really, it's all a bit much, isn't it?

So you go see trees but you're thinking of that figure who's waiting for you. And you take a photo of a raven by a castle wall and remember what you're on about. And you try to take a distracting photo of a castle and the city and a hill but it only does good for a little while because that hill reminds you of another hill where you were told stuff to do.

And so you just go to bed, because there's really no escape but sleep, and he's there again but this time it's much easier because you're starting to guess who he is.

17 December: Unfortunate Disclosures

So, I'm hanging off the side of a cliff-face talking to a giant, right? And it's kinda fucking scary because I'm this puny little man hanging onto the side of a mountain above a slightly-less-than-sheer 100 foot drop, and above me is the stone I'm trying to get to because it's white and carved and shouldn't be either of those things and actually, I'm kinda terrified remembering this stuff right now.

You do some crazy stuff when they tell you to, but you know what's crazier than climbing when you're no good at climbing and you made clear to your friend you had to do this yourself so you're all alone? Asking them for help.

And crazier still? Them saying 'yes.'

We went to Beddgelert, a small and brutally picturesque village in Snowdon. We'd originally planned on hitting the dark ford path of Snowdon ("Rhyd Ddu"), but a quick Ogham reading made me change my mind.

Beddgelert looks like what Thomas Kinkaid and the maker of every medieval fantasy video game tries to conjure on canvas or screen. In fact, you can play Skyrim, or go to Snowdon. One's cheaper and soul deadening, the other gets you a little rainy and wet and has real giants.

If you ever go, the story of Gelert (a dog mistakenly killed by his owner after saving a child from a wolf) is a bit of a ruse. Look underneath you when you go to his grave, and make sure you say hello, 'cause you'll need their permission.

And then you walk, or we walked, along the river's course. The wrong direction turns often enough into the correct direction if you're giving attention.

There's a nymph there in the water; I don't know what they're called in Welsh, but she likes cedar trees from cliff-faces. I'd say, "Fuck with her and I'll get quite angry," but she's hidden by her metaphor, which is how they all hide, yeah?

But if you ever go and want help finding her and are on about the right things, I'd help you find her. But the giant thing?

Oh, the giant thing.

Fuck metaphors.

A few months ago I was told what I'm on about. I mean, besides the Anarcho-Anti-Capitalist poetic musings that I thought I was on about I'm also on about that, you should know, but there's this other thing that I've been on about and I had to ask a giant (well, several, as I suspect word gets around with them quite well) if they'd help me.

They already have, I should say. Last year there was one rummaging through my head; another strode above me and then there were wild boars rummaging through my tent. And then another one punched someone for me. All metaphor, sure, if you need it to be because I don't need it to be any longer.

And they said yes, which is pretty damn cool of them. Giants are freaking awesome, even as you're pretty certain you're gonna lose your grip on the tree you're hanging on to and fall and then your best friend will find you with a broken neck.

But I didn't, because I'm writing you.

We then went to Llyn Dinas. Nearby is a place called Dinas Emrys, another 2000 year old fort said to be where Merlin released two imprisoned dragons. Another place is rumored to be nearby, the city of the Fferllyt (Druidic alchemists) from whom Ceridwen learned how to brew the potion of Awen.

So, pretty much kinda hardcore magic everywhere.

What I did there will unfold, who I met I'll get to know, what I carry I'll learn to use.

But what I've seen's been seared kinda deeply on the soul, like tattoos inked in wyrd. That's probably a metaphor, but probably not.

And I love you all.

A Kindness of Ravens (Travel Journals, IV)

Of all the stories I've become and the stories I've seen, the novels and narratives of these last few days are the most difficult to unravel.

Before I continue, though–I should remind you: the tales of the everyday are themselves quite profound. You, reading this at home perhaps, or surreptitiously at work, stealing a bit of your time back from your employer at a desk or behind a counter, may not perhaps see the stories around you, but they're there. It's not easy to read and retell 'em, but threads of narratives come loose easily from the fabric of the everyday when you pull hard enough, and you can re-weave a life from all those loose strands. It's just a little more difficult.

You just need to find a way to slip out of time where you stand, slip into the world between the walls, that older, persistent, ever-present world just outside where you are.

It's a bit easier to do on pilgrimage, of course. You leave all the things which create and sustain you in the wild hope you'll find what you don't quite know you're looking for. You become The Fool, dancing out into The World, stumbling upon mysteries in foreign lands.

There's a strange thing here, though. Sometimes the inhabitants of those foreign lands, neighbors to great mysteries and co-habitants with ancient gods of land, can't see what you're there to find. Perhaps it isn't really all that strange—if we, before we travel, have failed to see the magic around us in our mundane lives of work/home/consume/sleep, then even those living next to Cathedrals and shrines might miss the forest-in-the-wardrobe for the coat-tree.

The rationalist, certain only of the mundane, might say the Pilgrim is deluded, the Traveler mis-led, the Supplicant too certain of their visions to see the Real before them. "Look," they might say. "There's no magic here in this land–I've lived here my entire life."

They, ensconced upon their thrones, the land about them wasted, are the Fisher-King.

This is an odd thing: the Pilgrim then is Perceval, traveling through barren lands made whole against the unasked question.

Opening the dis-used, rusty, overgrown gates of the Other in the lands they visit, the pilgrim must return, bearing mystic keys to unlock the gates of home.

But I don't really want to return.

18 December: By Water and By Fire

Leaving Wales was the hardest thing I've done. It was so difficult that I haven't really done so.

Still when I close my eyes I'm standing at the narrow vale, about to step over to Llyn Dinas. Rivers pour from every stone around me, I'm immersed in clear flowing glass as Heather and Fern dance low to the ground in fierce, otherworldly winds.

I'm there, and I do not think I shall ever leave.

I'm also elsewhere. I'm on a bench in Berlin by a canal, under a Willow.

I'm in a cornfield near the top of an ancient Druid mountain in Bretagne as the full moon shines through thin clouds.

I'm by a river in the Hoh rainforest on the Olympic peninsula, drinking tea as the sun sets chill.

And I'm sitting in the darkness of my forest grove in Seattle, watching the flicker of a candle dance upon Fern and Maple from its setting within a Cedar stump, just as I'm watching candle-light shine fierce dragon-fire through raindrops on a bent Fir above Llyn Dinas.

I'm also in Dublin.

The Ferry from Wales to Dublin leaves from Holyhead on the Isle of Anglesy, and I'd planned to roam the Isle for several hours before taking an early evening sailing. A storm had risen upon the Irish Sea, though, and I'd been informed the night before: that ferry had been canceled.

So, the morning of the 19th Nick and I woke, ate breakfast and packed. We were both out-of-sorts; one doesn't just nonchalantly depart a place after several days of profound, ancient magic. Too, leaving Caernarfon together meant we'd soon leave each other, he on to Shrewsbury before returning to Cardiff, I on to Dublin before crossing a vast ocean.

We sat upon the sea-wall overlooking the Strait of Menai as the wind tore through our clothes, he clutching his hat, I trying to keep my hood over my head. Ravens and Gulls played upon those winds above us as we stared out towards Anglesy, unable to find many words.

When the time arrived, we boarded a bus to Bangor, and I taught him how to braid his beard. It's a strange thing for two men to do on a public bus, likely, though the working-class man behind us remarked only that he thought his own hands were too large and clumsy to braid a beard, so it's better he shaves his.

In Bangor, Nick and I departed. There's not much to say at that point, and despite being a bold extrovert given to spinning words and tales from a mere thought, there's a deep gift in the silence of a friend who knows what you'd say if it were needed, so you can eschew words altogether.

The Isle of Anglesy is not yet for me; this much was made clear by the storm and the land itself, only a place to pass through and hear the gathered voices chattering from the holy mount there. It has a Welsh name, one familiar to those who've heard the medieval-metal band Eluvietie. It is Ynys Môn, or Ins Mona.

It was the gate by which I entered, and the gate by which I needed to leave, but my shaking soul quaked my body as I boarded the ferry, watching in awe as oaths spewed from my lips like breath, as if summoned or extracted, pulled from me by the cords which now bind me to a land into which I'd almost disintegrated, atomized into the rain stars sun clouds stones trees streams in the service of the Blessed Raven.

I was bereft upon that ferry, a new Stygian journey.

I fear I've become like Orpheus, treading into the depths before I may return to the land of the living. That the whole world might become Hades after Gwynedd is perhaps unfair, but experience is not always just.

Just as I did not return from a night slept in crossroads on Menez Hôm unbroken, I did not return to Dublin quite the same. Raven feathers and old bones whip past my soul on winds I cannot now quell, and I fear I shall be always uneasy until my return.

19 December: Not Losing One's Head

My first night of sleep again in Dublin was a bit troubled, a different dread haunting me than the wild ancient giants of Snowdon had distilled into my soul from the lakes and stones.

After such high, fantastic, mist-soaked magic-days, I didn't know how to comprehend this. Gwynedd was so giving, so convivial and generous, laughing mirthfully with my feeble and awkward gestures that Ireland seemed suddenly *hostile.*

I've this funny quirk. I've never quite caught on to that strange thing about people, that some just seem really not to like each other and will never get along. I tolerate even the most frightful boors and aggressive idiots, and I've really less patience than I could have. It seems so easy, then, that I too-often forget that some will just always hate others and those sympathetic with them.

I've had plenty of evidence to convince me otherwise. Write something glowing about someone's writing and another writer declares a crusade against you. Be kind to one person and a whole host of others look upon you with suspicion. But even still, I forget.

My host and I left Dublin by bus for Brú na Bóinne, the Valley of the Boyne, a little after noon and arrived at 3pm. I'd been full of anticipation for this part of my journeys: the next morning, we'd be inside Newgrange to witness the dawning Solstice light.

Last year, when I arrived in Carnac, France, I fought hard the whim to throw off my rucksack and tear madly along the ancient tracks to the sacred wells and standing stones. The moment I arrived in Wales, nothing could prevent my gaping awe and manic laughter upon seeing the land before me. But upon my first step off the bus in the village of Donore, I wanted to vomit and then jump back on the bus, begging the quickest return to Dublin possible.

For many in America, Ireland is a sort of paradise, a lost Eden. Like Jerusalem for the Jewish Diaspora, Ireland has rooted itself deeply into the rich soil of a thousand dreams.

And I think it is indeed that place for which so many long. The smoke of glowing peat in a hundred hearths smells as you hope it does, the rolling hills, the mountains worn-low and soft just as you dream of them. The ancestors and Faeries and gods are most certainly and undeniably there, alive, strong and brooding and powerful and treacherously denied.

A Kindness of Ravens

Nothing will make you more certain of the existence of a god then the feeling of his land revolting against each of your steps, attempting to shake you off into the abyss of sky, twisting everything inside you into brutal knots, telling you to get out.

I wish I could tell you of the beauty of the land there, but I am not an objective observer. It's pretty, certainly. Go see it yourself, unless you've oathed yourself to someone who is unwelcome there.

I checked with my companion–he felt nothing askew, no strange dread. We checked into an inn at Donore, and when I'd learned he'd reserved it for two days I panicked. I wasn't sure I could survive more than a few hours in the place, let alone two nights.

We ate, and I felt no better.

The day was quite young, a few hours remaining of winter sunlight. In any other circumstances, I'd go exploring, visit and greet the streams and trees, but I felt such a crushing weight I thought the clear sky would suffocate me.

A graveyard stood within sight–the dead are generally reliable guides, and those I truck with are keen to introduce me. I told my companion I'd go consult them, and I managed only one step in that direction before turning forcefully about-face. The dead belonged to another, to the power of the land forbidding my passage.

I hid in our rented room and decided to nap. I've only once needed to ward the bed upon which I've slept. I don't even need to lock my house-doors in most places I've lived, yet I knelt, trembling, placing the strongest gate-stones I possess (grove stones, enchanted at the four cross-quarter gates) and slept, fully clothed, clutching the wand of Alder washed up upon the shores off Caer Arianrhod.

It felt as safe as sleeping in a blanket fort behind a couch as a child while your parents are fighting.

My companion woke me for dinner and I opened eyes, alert as if I hadn't slept. We ate at the inn, the sort of place done up more fancy than its cuisine. I couldn't shake my unease, one foot always bent from the floor, ready to spring from the table and run from the land.

It was maddening. Only once before have I felt so assaulted by the very air around me, last year, encountering the dead for the first time during Anaesterion. That time, I'd decided to check myself in to the psychiatric ward of a Seattle hospital and had called a foul-mouthed Thracian priest to inform him that I'd likely be gone awhile until he replied, laughing–

"Ah. Wear a hat."

"A hat? I think I'm gonna kill myself and you want me to wear a hat?"

"Yup," he'd replied, and I'm sure I heard him swig rum through the phone. "Do it and see how you feel. Check yourself in if you need to, but put on a hat, first."

He was...right. The hat quieted everything immediately, bought me enough time to douse myself in Florida Water (you're supposed to dilute that stuff, I guess...I didn't) and sleep in safety.

So I consulted him again, as well as a priest of The Morrígan and an Oracle crafted by a friend, and their combined answers told me what I couldn't uncover in my maddened state:

The Dagda wasn't quite pleased at my presence, and if you've read The Mabinogion and know why I'm a bit corvid-obsessed, you'll know why.

Newgrange is said to belong to The Dagda, and know what? It's very much his.

This time I couldn't just put on a hat. Dark beer, dirt-money, my taste into the ground for passage; the same amount of dirt-money on leaving. By the time I discovered all this, the inn's bar was about to close, so I hastened there, broodingly searching out a beer. The place was crowded, the patrons all linked, cut from the same bolts of cloth, laughing and moving almost as one as I pushed through them, unyielding.

It's not uncommon to find yourself in such situations, a shifting labyrinth (indeed, it happened the next day) until you've bought your passage through, or at least greeted the Presence re-arranging the world around you, preventing you everywhere.

Also, it's hard to do ritual in public, even in a bar. In Seattle I tip out libations from my first beer of the night upon the floor when I'm out—adding up the spirits and gods for whom these are given, most of my first pint is empty before it's my turn for a sip. But here? Not a good idea.

Of course, shoving a coin in your mouth and walking outside with a mouthful of beer looks a bit suspicious, too, even to drunk folks, but it was the easier route.

The moment I got outside and spit the beer-soaked coin onto the ground, everything lightened. I returned to my beer inside, and found myself suddenly engaged in conversation with a damn hot man named Liam. He had things to tell me, that drunken straight-man confessional where he's leaning on me, his mouth too close to my ear not to arouse, telling me tales of why he had to leave.

"Grew up here," he said. "Just down the road, by Newgrange. No jobs, y'know. I'm a carpenter," he added, as I resisted fetishizing his profession and his scruffy jaw. "But the work's in London. There's shit here."

And then he wandered off, and I could not stop thinking about the children of The Dagda, his Cauldron of plenty just nearby, but his name never called.

20 December: Threading the Eyeless Rocks

Newgrange is but a 30 minute walk from the village of Donore, but we woke early. I don't think I could have slept much longer. My passage was bought for a short time; another god had spoken on behalf of me, it appeared, one I barely know but consider quite fondly–Lugh. His kindness confirms a suspicion a friend had last year that there's a connection between him and the resistance of peasants and workers, both in Ireland and nearby, seen particularly in the tales of the Luddites and their mysterious leader, King Ludd. A guard, explaining why they'd fallen back at the approach of Luddites destroying a factory, testified to a pale, shining warrior wielding a pike (i.e., a spear). Perhaps Lugh likes me because I'm advocating the same sort of struggle.

If anyone summoned me to witness a spear of sunlight streaming into a 5000 year old burial mound on the morning of the Winter Solstice, I'm suspecting it was him. There seems to be…some arrangement, I guess, between some gods, gods who are on about the same sorts of things. Lugh no doubt knew what I intend to do, as would Brighid, as I told her.

Even still, the last twenty minutes of the walk to Brú na Bóinne required the lighting of a candle offered to a certain very old being met on Llyn Dinas in order to even approach.

What whispered from the trees as we walked was not kind.

The moon rose in the east just as we arrived at the visitor's center, the sharpest crescent of Ceridwen I've seen in quite some time. It cheered me even as I noted its razor-edged sickle. Death is hardly an inconvenience, let alone a fear, and I was going to witness the moment modern Druids depict as the symbol of Rebirth.

The Brú na Bóinne visitor center is a bit of a trip in itself, as are the women who greet you with the most curious, knowing smiles as one of the randomly chosen few to witness the event. 50 are selected each year by school-children from five local primary schools. The odds are nearly impossible, except that all impossible odds are never actually impossible, otherwise they wouldn't be odds at all.

There's a sense that you're about to be initiated into something, though if any of the folks who work at the visitor center are devotees of an ancient religion, they most certainly don't let on. They seem like cheerful cafeteria ladies, asking if you'd like chocolate or regular milk (they even offer free breakfast after the event for the selected).

The light enters the tomb over a period of six days ("Solstice Vigil," our guide called it), and the previous few days had not been good. Newgrange isn't far from the sea, and the mists are known to come in to veil the site. There'd been a 6-year period where the sun hadn't been seen on any of those days: the luck afforded by chance selection could not, after all, guarantee a clear sunrise.

We sipped complementary tea and chewed on oat biscuits until the time came for us to be transported by bus to the foot of the mound upon which Newgrange sits. You cross a tributary of the Boyne to the bus-stand, board along with 21 other excited and nervous folks, and are released into the crowds of others lingering expectantly around the mound, those who come to witness the sunrise from outside the tomb.

Two things caught my eye as we walked the path to the entrance. As I passed a tree, it filled suddenly with an unkindness of Ravens, calling out fiercely in voices I recognized, voices familiar to me, calls and chants in solidarity.

The second? A man, sitting with his back against one of the stones surrounding the site, holding a wooden flute, staring at the east. I'd need to talk to him, I understood, but I didn't yet know why.

The moments before entering the passage were heady. Folks took photos of themselves almost as if to distract themselves from the tension and excitement rather than to mark the occasion. I mingled amongst them, listening to the fragments of their stories, their clipped speech, their tales caught short in the throat. There wasn't anything really to say, but they were about to walk into a tomb. Solemnity isn't needed before such a thing.

We were gathered by an announcement as others turned to watch us, we 22 people with our dinky lanyards and plastic passes suspended awkwardly around our necks. I watched the faces of those who wouldn't be able to enter, who hadn't been chosen. There was no envy or jealousy there, only expectation, an eagerness to hear from us what we would see.

And then we entered.

A Kindness of Ravens

Lights had been turned on to guide in; it's utterly dark otherwise, and I suspect otherwise they'd have quite a few injuries on their hands. The chamber was illuminated only long enough for us to enter and to stand with our backs against the wall, making a semi-circle, facing inward upon the path where, if the weather held, the spear of the sun would enter.

And then, darkness. The voice of the guide spoke, calming those who might have found themselves in fear at the blackness in the chamber. It's dark, indeed, and just beyond that darkness, what?

What the others saw and heard, I do not know. There was much chatter, nervous, curious questions eager to fill the silence. If one is an apt student of other humans, one need not possess sharp psychic powers to hear the Other—you need only listen to the edge in the voice of others, the muted, nervous laughter stifling a gasp or an ancient sigh, a groan hidden as a throat-clearing cough. When the throngs of dead enter a tavern or pass through a crowd, you can hear them in the echoes of clamor and laughter.

It is this for which the Sciences were made, observations of what is manifest upon the material. It is our loss it tries to explain the shadows of the light according to the patterns in its books. What the guide offered those assembled souls together was a calm, reasoned voice, like the bell or drum of the shaman, a guide-line along a blind path. The age of the structure, the science and maths of angles and rotation. One thinks of W.S. Merwin's poem, "The Widow"

There is no season
That requires us
Masters of forgetting
Threading the eyeless rocks with
A narrow light

But even in the guide's calming, reasoned voice you could hear her sudden gasp.

"Ah," she said, breathless. "Here it is."

We stood and watched. Some tentatively reached their hands to touch the light, hesitant, pulling their hands back suddenly as if afraid they'd done something profane or too sacred.

I can hear them all now; not the dead, but the living, their strange, wild joy, halting words trying to express what they saw. Other pilgrims from all over, bewildered and enchanted. No ritualist was present to make sense for them this occurrence; the "science" only ever goes so far, and what was left to them was the world of meaning, the event in itself the Thing and they, rebels, anarchists, staring into Lugh's spear, a light which 5000 years later has never gone out.

The magic is within the tomb, yes. But it's also when you leave.
The faces you meet when you exit the passage greet you into a new dawn, the Dawn of the year, the Dawn of the World. You are reborn with the sun, whether you died or not.

"You'll Know It When You See It"

There's one more story I need to tell you of this day, what happened before we fled swiftly as my time ran out, as the "dirt-money" I paid The Dagda would not permit me to miss the first bus out of Donore. I felt everything unravel, like a vampire racing the dawn perhaps, or a Raven fleeing a storm.

I was asked by many people to say prayers on their behalf, to collect soil or water or stones. It's what you do on Pilgrimage, carrying the wishes and dreams and good-will of others as a walking staff or a warm cloak against the chill. At Newgrange I uttered a prayer on behalf of my friend Lupus, as I arrived, as I entered, as the light shone, as I exited, and as I left. It's a beautiful prayer, one I was honored to utter on behalf of another.

A part of it required finding a certain "very interesting" stone behind the tomb, and as I made my way to it, I encountered another man standing before it, staring intently. It was the man I'd noted upon entering, the one I knew I must talk to.

"Hey," I said, fumbling in my pocket. The man turned, a bit startled, his eyes full of dream, his face seeing something else beyond what was before us.

"I need to give this to you," I said, finding the small yellow cloth I'd carried with me into the tomb. Of all the things I brought with me, it seemed the strangest and least relevant. A gift from my friend Alley Valkyrie, a patch printed with a bee.

I didn't quite know what I was doing as I handed it to him, I only knew I must. I could fight the silent command, but in the time of the Mysteries, there after being one of the few humans alive to witness the shaft of solstice light flood through a 5000 year-old tomb, resisting anything makes no sense.

A Kindness of Ravens

To be fair, it also made little sense that I needed to have the patch in the tomb with me, though I knew I must. No "reason" dictated that I lay it upon a stone as the light shone through, but there was no doubt when I did so.

"Uh," he said, awed. "I keep bees."

I could only smile, mutely, so he repeated himself, staring at the bee in his hand. "My wife and I keep bees. How did you know?"

I laughed, because I could do nothing else. "There you are, then. It's for you, from my friend Alley Valkyrie. Happy Solstice!"

He let me take his photo and gave me his name, John, and I proceeded to utter the next part of Lupus's prayer before the stone:

Paths well-worn have all here lead,
heavy deeds so far to tread;
join this world to other ones–
one night cloaking many suns.

And I could not stop laughing, neither at the power in those words before the stone, nor at Alley's request for my pilgrimage. I'd asked her what she would like on my travels, and she'd answered, only, "you'll know it when you see it."

And I'd smiled when I'd heard those words, because I've learned to know things when they're seen, a spear of light, the kindness of ravens, and the faces of the others all reflecting an awakening dream.

The Tomb of
the Atheist

I'm standing, dazed, along the shores of Lake Michigan, staring into my distant reflection in the parabolic, ethereal polished glass of the Cloud Gate.

The air's chill, icy—a thin layer of rime had begun to form that morning along the edges of the sand.

I'd stopped in Chicago to visit a man I love deeply, a man to whom a god had introduced me. I'd just spent several weeks traveling in Ireland and Wales, speaking to gods and meeting the dead, and this was the last stop of my pilgrimage before returning to Seattle.

The reflections in the Cloud Gate are fascinating, both distorted and yet hyper-realistic. It takes you awhile to pick yourself out of the throngs of others in the public square in which it sits, but once you do, it's hard to lose yourself again. It seems as if you're what the sky sees of you, rather than others. A strange perspective, but one you can get used to.

The man, who I'm waiting before the Cloud Gate for, appears with his partner. We don't know each other very well, have never met before, but it seemed we ought to meet. And I'm never in Chicago.

He smiles and introduces himself. And then, he places a gift in my hand.

"The only thing I could think of to give another Druid was an Acorn," he said.

A Kindness of Ravens

I held it, smiling. Here, in a sea of concrete, in the deepness of winter, my future quite unclear to me, I stare at the promise of an oak in my hand. It warmed me against the chill, grounded me into the world below the concrete.

I stood there, considering the acorn in my hand, the reflection of myself in that strange glass, and began to realize who had just died in a tomb in Ireland a week before.

I.

On a grey and beautiful September morning I had woken, smiling, and kissed my lover before stumbling out of bed and making tea. He'd been visiting me all month, a long visit to determine whether we'd work out living with each other, as he lived several thousand miles away.

I made my morning tea and checked email as I sipped it, waiting for the morning to come to consciousness. And then I spilled my tea.

"You won't believe this. I don't myself, either. Check your email—I've forwarded it to you."

My hand trembled, but not from excitement. Dread, perhaps. I knew what the email would say before I opened it. The friend who'd sent it would only have one reason to forward a message to me.

I opened it, scanned its words to confirm my terror, and then rolled several cigarettes, smoking each in turn until enough nicotine coursed through my brain to put me into that half-trance some smokers know quite well.

"Really?" I asked aloud, but no one answered, only a breathing, autumnal silence.

I waited to wake the beautiful man in my bed. The fur of his chest matted, his face peaceful, contentment radiating from his dreaming form. I wanted to watch him that way, perhaps keep him that way forever in my mind, stilled in the moment before I told him of my great fortune, fortune which we both knew, without saying, would make impossible many of our plans.

Even now, I see him sleeping there, before I nuzzled him awake, before I spoke the words which would change not just him and I, but everything else I knew.

II.

"I'm going to Newgrange."

The hiring manager looked at me. "What's that?"

"Uh. An ancient burial mound. Aligned with the sun, sorta. Um, solstice. It's in Ireland."

"Oh," he said. "That sounds cool. When—Oh. You can't start yet, then, huh?"

"Not unless you'd let me take a few weeks unpaid leave at the beginning of hire?"

"Uh—I think HR would say no. Maybe you can start when you return…"

That'd be nice, I thought. Though I'd been hoping to start sooner, returning to the full-time social work position I'd held before my…uh, last pilgrimage, the one that'd sent me away from Seattle for almost a year. I was back in Seattle, working per diem, happy to finally be sitting still, with a permanent address. Also, my lover planned to move in with me, and my writing was going well—I might finally get to do the sort of grown-up life that I'd had before gods started talking to me.

Returning to full-time social work would cut into my writing. To write well, and often, one requires unoccupied time, and lots of it. It's never just sitting in front of a computer and touching fingers against keys. It's about the walks to a forest in the middle of the night, the hours spent staring listlessly out of windows or watching incense smoke curl from glowing ember-tip. Sometimes it means getting drunk when you shouldn't or don't even want to. Lots of listening, thinking, with relentless false starts and stops. It's an awful lot of work, actually

But writing doesn't pay rent, or buy food, so you have to also work elsewhere. This is the plight of any artist, finding work that doesn't detract too much from art. Few ever find work which helps one's art, though such does exist—photographers who work in camera shops, potters and painters who take jobs as art teachers for access to kilns and cheap canvases.

Social work doesn't help writing, but it doesn't hurt it too much, either. On the worst days, it'll make you distrust humanity completely, but on the better days, one at least goes home with a vague sense of having done something less horrible than what one could have.

Full-time job, a lover to become a partner—this is what I'd been hoping for, working towards, ready to embrace. Enough money to survive in the brutal inflationary city of Seattle and perhaps a little to save. Maybe I'd join a gym, get my teeth fixed, purchase a third pair of trousers and a second pair of shoes. Even, I'd hoped, I might start my medieval rock band again, the one I broke up when the gods came and....

Uh, yeah. I've been here before. Even the lover bit.

III.

The Druid who handed me the acorn before the Cloud Gate asked me a question I didn't quite answer fully. He'd asked about the gods, stating he hadn't done much with them and wasn't sure he would. They seem to demand a lot, he'd suggested, but it was also a question.

My answer sounded pretty, anyway. "If land spirits, the dead, and ancestors are all like notes in a symphony, a god is the melody."

Pretty, but untrue.

A god's like all the music written upon the pages of your existence, all the songs you hear wherever you go, each melody and each refrain. You are their instruments and they are the reason you're sitting in a chair before a conductor in front of thousands of silent strangers straining to hear your notes.

Gods re-order the world around you, shut fast doors and destroy keys as if to say, "you won't need these anymore. We've other places for you to go." And then they hand you new keys and show you new doors to take you to different places that you'd never even considered visiting.

One of those places, apparently, was Newgrange.

The email from a friend that morning in late September was a forwarded message from the Brú na Bóinne visitor center, announcing I'd been selected by local schoolchildren for a chance to observe the Winter Solstice light from within the tomb. Access to Newgrange is relatively open the rest of the year—anyone can go and be part of the guided tours into the 5000-year old tomb. Lights are turned off during the guided tour, and artificial lights are shone into the chamber to mimic the effect which occurs the five mornings adjacent to and including the Winter Solstice.

The phenomena was rediscovered in 1967 by the archaeologists who'd taken it upon themselves to restore the ancient burial site. Knowledge of the alignment of the entrance to the Winter Solstice sun persisted much longer, encoded in folk tales. Archeologists and anthropologists are unfortunately known for ignoring the oral accounts of the peoples they study. But time and again, letting the stories of peoples inform academia rather than the other way around restores truth to the world.

It's said that the smallpox vaccine, for instance, was developed after a researcher heard and then observed the folk custom of rubbing the pus of cox-pox wounds into the skin of children. The researcher gets credit for the "discovery," as this is how The Science works.

The Science can tell us lots about how things work or how they were done, but it begins to look quite ridiculous when it starts to try to tell us "why." Why did the inhabitants of Ireland, some five millennia ago, build a massive (and enduring) tomb in the valley of the Boyne river and align it to the rising sun one day a year? Why Stonehenge? Why the pyramids, or ziggurats, or colossal statues along the Nile or on Easter Isle?

Theories abound, and The Science is faddish. The Science hasn't quite stopped doing lobotomies yet, but that exciting trend is happily almost over, replaced with chemicals to "right" what's wrong with the brain when people start talking to gods or the dead. What comes next is as unpredictable as next decade's hair fashions, and as permanent. Perhaps Newgrange, too, was faddish, like Neuro-linguistics is now?

Another thing The Science cannot quite explain were the emails that my friend Joseph sent me from Dublin. "I saw you in Dublin today, at least five times."

I'd read that email 8 months before, after work in Eugene, Oregon. It was a curious thing. I wasn't in Dublin, nor had I been before. It's never been unusual for people to think they saw me, and even less unusual for others to recount vivid dreams involving me. My best friend dreamt of "Druid Rhyd" years before I decided to study Druidry; another friend told me where to find a god because he recalled me telling him later where I found him. I'm accustomed to such things and think little of them. One can only shrug when someone tells you that they taught you to shapechange in their dreams and remind them that you haven't quite gotten the hang of it yourself yet.

The week after Joseph thought he saw me, he put my name in to the drawing for Sostice in Newgrange. He didn't put his own name in, though he could have. He never quite explained to me why this was, nor why he did it in the first place.

It was to him they'd sent the selection email. 30 thousand others had put their names in hopes of attending, and only 50 are selected each year. Each selectee is allowed to bring a guest, and the 100 total attendees are divided up into three groups to be inside the tomb either December 20th, the 21st, or 22nd. I was invited to the first of the three days, not "Solstice" per se, but Druidry's taught me enough about the precision to know we humans care a little too much for it.

So I was selected to go. I hadn't put my name in. I'd never planned to go to Ireland, despite how many others had suggested I ought to, despite the voice of an Irishman met on my last pilgrimage, showing me his tattoos and insisting that I "must go" to Newgrange one day.

The selection was exciting, and also eerie. One can't go attributing every bit of strange fortune to the gods, of course.

One also can't go not attributing bizarre bits of fortune to the gods, either, at least if you've gone about worshiping them and telling them you'll do what they'd like.

IV.

Going to Ireland would mean not taking the full-time job I'd been offered. I wouldn't be able to get the approval for unpaid time off during the holidays, and they couldn't start me early enough to have sufficient paid-time for the trip.

I'd also intended to help my lover with expenses for the move to Seattle. We'd planned on the first of December, but this would mean he'd be in a new city on his own during the week of Christmas while I traipsed about ancient holy sites without him. And I would already have to do a fundraiser to pay for the trip, as last-minute tickets to Ireland during the holidays aren't something my income could ever hope to cover.

I'd asked a diviner about a different matter, a question I'd not been able to answer on my own. She hadn't known about the Newgrange trip, but had mentioned Lugh had my attention for some reason.

"Huh," I'd said. "So I just got selected to go to Newgrange in Ireland. I can't afford to go, but maybe…"

"Oh, you're going," she said, and her laughter almost scared me. "That much is very, very certain."

The next day I started a fundraiser, an Indigogo "campaign" and asked for 500 dollars. I raised that in the first 4 days, and received another 500 the next week.

So—I was going.

My employer suggested they might be able to hold the position open for me, though it'd be more likely I'd have to take a different and less desirable one if not. My lover seemed willing to move upon my return instead.

All would be in place, then. I'd return poor and full of stories to a secure job and an end to the geographical distance of a man I'd loved for most of a year.

One likes the idea of the world being in order before doing something you know will otherwise send everything into upheaval. Before I do a ritual that I suspect will re-order my brain a bit and before I go to speak to gods that I do not know well, I clean my room, make my bed, do laundry. I check to make sure I've enough tea for afterward, food waiting for me when it's all over, or a safe and quiet evening awaiting me. The Other is disruptive; this I've learned quite well. Returning from the Other to this world is easier when there are no chores to do, no pressing concerns awaiting at the other end.

The night before I left, my lover told me he was not ready to move. The specifics were unimportant—underlying the reason was an unspoken statement, the unacknowledged hesitancy which makes easily-surmountable obstacles suddenly impossible to overcome.

Suddenly, going to Newgrange seemed the most unreasonable thing I could possibly have chosen to do, and it wasn't even my idea in the first place.

V.

I woke at 5am the morning of my flight, hefted a rucksack full of books and clothes, stones, an altar box, gifts for people along the way. I was 'told' I didn't need to pack certain things, like my alder wand. "One will be provided for you," I'd heard. I played with the words, waited to see if they changed. They repeated, the same tone and certainty as before. So I left it on my altar, perplexed.

"But bring the bee."

I stared at the yellow and white patch in my hands. I'd meant to sew it on my coat months before, soon after it was given to me. I was never certain why I'd waited, put it off. I've many intentions like this, intentions I rarely find the time to manifest. But perhaps I'd find a needle and thread along the way? So I placed it, without much thought, in my wooden altar box before packing it into my giant rucksack.

I stayed a few days in Florida with family before leaving to Dublin. I'd visited them last year at the end of a pilgrimage; it seemed poetic to visit them again just before the next.

My sisters and I laughed and talked and ate, catching each other up on our lives and hopes. They'd been as perplexed and amazed as I was regarding the Newgrange selection. "It seems really weird, right?" I'd asked. "The probability of getting chosen without even putting in your name…"

They understood, agreed. Though I'd met no one who had shrugged off the serendipity of the trip, and even my more cynical friends had suggested it seemed "something wants you there," without reference to other people's conceptions of causation, the mystic becomes forced to rely on self-generated checks against magical thinking.

These artificial "devil's advocates" can be ridiculous, a caricature of the angry and cynical voices of others. Mine has the arrogant certainty of Richard Dawkins, the drunken wit of Christopher Hitchens, and the pop-appeal of Neil DeGrasse Tyson, a curmudgeon with a grudge always eager to tell me, "that's not a god—you need psych meds. And oh, you're poor because you're lazy."

But even that compound, inner atheist naysayer was having trouble convincing me this wasn't all about what I'd suspected it was, and the perspective of my sisters demolished all my inner cynic's attempts. They knew what we came from, the abject poverty and misery, all the heavy leaden weight of fate crushing every dream. When you've seen all the horrible things which can happen to a human, every nice thing already seems a miracle. Perhaps it's why the poor, the homeless, the downtrodden and miserable are more likely to believe in gods and spirits than the middle-class lawyer or IT worker. Voltaire's atheism was as elitist as Sam Harris's, and both have enjoyed steady diets.

Still. I liked that atheist in my head. Unlike Harris and Dawkins, he didn't justify the torture of Muslims and suggest we should eradicate Islam off the face of the planet. He mostly just told me I'm insane and should be more reasonable and stop believing in crazy stuff and go shopping for nicer clothes.

VI.

The first thing I noticed about Dublin was the dead.

I didn't always hear the dead and wasn't always aware of their presence. I have the city of Eugene, Oregon, the grave of Demetria and Dionisia Palazios, and a Guédé that I met under an Elm tree to thank for that, as well as a drunken Thracian priest, who helped me stay on this side of the living after I met them.

The streets of Dublin breathe the dead. Signs point the way to famous graves of revolutionaries and poets, but there's no clear marking for the Croppies Acre along the River Liffey. You hear them before you find out why, what the large field before you precisely is: a mass grave of Revolutionaries, Republican fighters, their bodies dumped together in pits by the British. When we think "mass grave," we like to kid ourselves that such things happen in "other lands," though, we in America are virtually living upon one.

The connection between starved and slaughtered 'indian' and starved and slaughtered Irish-folk isn't hard to make; if anything, it's awfully hard to ignore. The dead scream, too, in the signs and graffiti smeared across the city proclaiming more revolution, more resistance, this time directed against the very system which drives colonial occupations for the last 300 years.

Dublin isn't far from Brú na Bóinne, a 45 minute bus ride away. I'd traveled already several thousand miles to get to Ireland, had just taken a several day detour to view Caer Arianrhod and speak to giants near the ancient Welsh town of Beddgelert, so the bus-ride from Dublin to the village of Donore wasn't long at all.

Still. That dread that I had felt when I first learned of my selection returned, this time accompanied by a spiraling, physical terror upon stepping foot off the bus.

My inner Atheist had little to say about the matter. "Maybe you need a nap, that's all. There's no god here."

He was always saying stuff like that.

I slept with my clothes on, clutching an Alder wand that washed up on shore by Caer Arianrhod in Wales.

"You know Brân attacked the Irish, right?" This was a priest talking, one I'd hoped might explain to me why the earth seemed to want to shake me off into the sky around Brú na Bóinne.

"Yeah," I assented. "But it was their fault."

"Still—" he replied, rather patiently. "Newgrange is the home of The Dagda, and, well…"

Another priest I asked confirmed my dread. "You have to buy passage. Dirt money, beer, spit. Pay the same on the way out. Someone will help you–you know who, I don't."

And I checked a third oracle, just because my inner Atheist was having fits. "His mother's body lies rotting in the summer ground."

Neil Dawkins Harris was gritting his teeth. It was actually interesting to hear from him again, though, as he'd seemed to have gotten lost on the ferry ride to Wales and wasn't with me when I climbed 100 feet up a cliff face to ask some giants for help rebuilding the Cult of the Blessed Raven. He wasn't there when Bran showed up to me in a dream and told me he'd be waiting after this was all over. He'd been silent when a Druid pulled my beard and wouldn't let go until I pulled his back.

I had three confirmations from others. Three other people didn't think I was crazy.

Druids like threes.

I bought a beer, put a coin in my mouth, swished the beer around and then spit it all out on the ground, asking the Dagda for passage, and reminded him that the god who's mother lied rotting in the summer fields had called me there in the first place.

My inner atheist was awfully pissed at me, more than The Dagda had been.

VII.

Reason told me that I'd done an awfully silly thing—maybe even a crazy thing. One doesn't just risk a relationship and one's livelihood to go on a pilgrimage to try to resurrect a god's cult. Nor does one beg strangers for the money to do so.

Joseph and I talked a lot about this sort of thing while he hosted me in Dublin. He was as shocked as I about the selection, and I relied heavily on his narrative to help place my own. He moved to Dublin last year to work in IT. He doesn't like IT, didn't know anyone in Dublin before taking the job. Didn't quite even know why he put my name instead of his for the drawing.

His best friend had died recently, and it's a strange new thing about what I've been on about lately that I'm aware of dead spirits clinging closely to the living. His beloved friend wasn't far, and I accepted quietly how much she was present to him when I was near. She and I even shared a birthday, and were both social workers.

Joseph didn't suffer the same animosity from The Dagda as I did. But he probably suffered overmuch from my panic at being there. Because I could take a guest into Newgrange with me, I took him. It seemed the gods wanted him there as much they wanted me there.

We walked that morning mostly in silence to the Brú na Bóinne visitor center, joining 20 other groggy but excited people awaiting something very few humans ever get the chance to try to see. And it was a chance, of course—there's never a guarantee the sun will shine into the tomb on solstice morning, on account of clouds. There'd recently been a 6-year stretch where none of the visitors saw what Joseph and I got to see that morning.

We ate cookies and drank tea and waited for the bus that would drive us to Newgrange. Others had gone on ahead; those who hadn't won the drawing but still wanted a chance to watch the sun rise from outside.

The awkward anticipation of the others in our group was as exhilarating as my own excitement. Listening to strangers speak of what may come, how they'd been chosen, how they'd never dreamt of such a chance filled me with such warmth that I almost didn't care if the sun would rise that morning. Gods written on the faces and the lips of others are as present as those whispering in dreams, and more tangible.

When we arrived at the site of Newgrange, Joseph and I walked silently up the hill, both turning at once to stare at the hundreds of corvids, which had taken to a barren tree just at the base of the mound. I'd told him of Brân and what I'd been doing in Wales. He smiled, wordlessly, and I was glad of a witness even as my inner atheist stamped his feet angrily, reminding me I'd have a lot more money if I stopped buying peanuts to feed crows in Seattle.

Just outside the tomb was a man who drew my attention immediately. I noticed my hand rubbing the fabric of the bee patch in my pocket, the one that I ran back into our hotel room to grab because I heard a voice say I'd need it.

And then we entered.

VIII.

It's dark inside a tomb.

We were led in by a guide who kindly walked us through what we might see, her voice assuring us in the darkness once the lights had been extinguished. We were allowed no photography, since it would distract from the experience of others, but she encouraged us to speak to each other, adding that she'd kindly guide anyone out who experienced any sudden terror in the claustrophobic blackness in which we huddled.

She spoke of the history of Newgrange; what The Science knows and particularly what The Science doesn't know. She spoke fondly of the archeologist – the one who had confirmed that the folk stories about the chamber becoming illuminated in the Solstice sunrise, and then she reminded us that it was not certain we'd see it.

"There was no light yesterday. We keep solstice vigil for 6 days each year, and I've only seen it a handful of times since I started working here."

And then her voice caught in her throat. "Ah," she said, all awe. "Here we are."

Just at sunrise, the angle of the sun shines into a small window-box above the entrance to the tomb. From inside, one cannot quite see this window due to the angles of the construction, nor can one see the exit from within the inner chamber. We stood in complete darkness, and then suddenly, just as she spoke, the thinnest shaft of light, a spear of sun, shot through the window into the chamber.

I still feel that great, collective inhalation of the gathered crowd huddled in the tomb at that first thin needle of light. There was nothing to say, nothing to understand, nothing to be done except watch.

The light grew, and as it did a few people put out their hands to touch it, tentatively. They seemed so hesitant, unsure if it was appropriate, uncertain what it might do or mean. One could almost hear their inner atheists thumbing copies of Stephen Pinker's latest drivel as mine was, but then, like a storm, the exuberance released, acceptance descended, and we basked in the sight.

It was difficult to see what others were doing, but I noticed, just to my right, a man put on a pair of glasses that were not his. I'd seen those glasses–they were on Joseph's mantle, next to the picture of his deceased friend. They'd belonged to her, and he'd put them on to gaze upon the light with her eyes, to see the way she might have seen, and perhaps to help her see, too.

IX.

I left my inner atheist impaled upon Lugh's shining spear in that tomb.

Outside the tomb, the voices were raucous, full of joy and wonder. Those outside waited word from we who'd been within to hear what it was like. We who'd been inside tried to find the words to describe what we'd seen to faces full of as much wonder as we.

Behind the tomb, I found the man I was supposed to find. He was standing in front of a stone that a friend had asked me to say a prayer before, and so I waited until he moved, my hand clutching the fabric in my pocket.

There was no voice to tell me "no" any longer, no inner atheist to chide me for entertaining such ridiculous thoughts.

I said hello to him. "Hey–I…can I give this you? I'm supposed to, I think."

The man looked at the patch in his hand. "It's a bee."

I nodded. "Yeah. It's from my friend Alley Valkyrie."

"I keep bees," he said, his face unreadable.

Of course he keeps bees, I thought to myself. That's why it's for him. "It's definitely for you, then. Happy Solstice."

Joseph and I left Newgrange soon after. I had to, as The Dagda had made it clear I was to take the first bus out.

I got what I'd came for, though, saw what I needed to see. I'd recited the prayers I'd been asked to, delivered the bee I'd been directed to by unseen voices I've learned to trust much more than the suddenly silent, sadly deceased corpse of my inner atheist.

I figured The Dagda could use some overly-reasonable company for a little while.

The Disenchanted
Kingdom

Once upon a time, an evil wizard wanted to enslave the world. He really didn't have any good reason to enslave people, except he was a very lazy evil wizard and didn't want to do stuff for himself. Also, he liked shiny things, and nice things, and liked to be comfortable.

Other evil wizards were trying to enslave the world, too, but they only managed to enslave bits of it. A small kingdom here, a large village there, but not the entire world. Worse, none of the wizards could hold onto their slaves for very long. They'd keep escaping, or would throw the wizards out of towers. And this made all the evil wizards sad, because though they were powerful, a pitchfork through the stomach really ruined their day.

This evil wizard had a name, but he cast a spell of forgetting and so I don't remember it. Do you remember it? No?

Then the spell worked.

One day, the evil lazy wizard whose name we all forgot was half-squatting with his robe hiked above his waist. He was waiting for his slaves to finish rubbing soft white paper on his butt cheeks when he had an idea.

He had wondered why no wizards had enslaved the entire world, and he thought he could succeed where they failed, because he took Success

Magic Seminars and learned to believe in himself and trust in his own laziness.

"No one wants to be a slave," he thought to himself, waiting for his slaves to finish. He was looking through the window of his tower as they wiped him. He liked to see the fields where people toiled in fear of him, planting and harvesting and baking and sewing and forging for him. But he knew those people hated him, and he knew they wanted to kill him, and he knew that he wasn't immortal, and this made him a very sad, evil wizard.

And then he realized what he needed to do.

So he summoned the other evil wizards. He hated them, he wanted their slaves and wealth, but he needed their help. Also, they ate all his food when they came over, because they were very greedy wizards like him.

So they all sat in his very spacious tower, around a bespoke African Blackwood barn-door table inlaid with black Rhino horn and discussed the problem.

"Our slaves want to kill us," he said, as they all grumbled suspiciously at him, keeping one hand on their wands. But no one disagreed with him.

"And we're afraid of them, right?" He had his hand on his own wand, too–he wasn't gonna be in a room full of wizards holding their wands without gripping his own, larger and thicker wand.

A few of the other evil wizards shouted back.

"I fear no one!" roared one wizard, making the chainmail under his wizard's robes rattled.

"They are ignorant and powerless!" shouted another, stroking the intricately-carved arcane fire-wand he'd forced an artisan to make for him.

"They are lazy and greedy!" said a third, patting his over-full stomach so hard the heavy purse of gold hanging from his belted-robe jangled.

"We should kill them all!" said a fourth, rather stupid wizard.

Everyone stared at him and glowered, gripping their wands tighter.

"They are all those things, yes," said the first evil wizard. "But we need them, because without them we'd have to do things for ourselves, and who here even knows how to clean your butt?"

Silence and intense introspective stares filled the room, followed by expressions of confusion, disgust, and finally utter panic.

"You get my point, then," the first wizard said, and the other wizards nodded, fiercely.

"But our slaves don't want to be slaves, and they're always trying to stop slaving, and just yesterday Gurdlebuff the Greasy was thrown from his tower by a group of women-slaves."

The other wizards choked with the news. Gurdlebuff had been a very powerful wizard, and very, very lazy. Though they were happy to lose a competitor, they all knew that if the slaves could kill ol' Greasy, they could kill them, too.

"We have to do something!" exclaimed a shrill wizard named Anadora the Vain. She looked like a wedding cake, with white-frilled robes with pink-and-beige trim, and the powder on her face when she sweat looked thick and clumpy, like frosting. "Just the other day I saw a one of my slave-women wearing something pretty! How dare they? And you know what comes next? They'll decide they can love whoever they want and think they can choose how many new slaves they birth for me!"

A great uproar rose from the other wizards, shouts of "we can't have that!" and "how dare they!" and even "kill all the women-slaves!"

It took awhile for the crowd to settle.

"So," said their host, smoothing his robes. "You are all agreed–we must find a new way to control our workers."

The wizard with the chain-mail under his robes protested. "Slaves!" he said, quite angrily. "They're our slaves."

"Serfs!" cried another, and "peasants" shouted a third until the whole room erupted with more shouts. It was very, very loud.

But suddenly, they all went quiet, because their host was known for a horrible temper.

"They are all those things, yes. But we will now call them our workers. If they think they are slaves, they will try to rise up and throw us out our windows and off our chamberpots. We must change, and use a new magic to control them."

Everyone in the room clutched their wands tightly, though some started stroking them a bit, whispering things to the wooden shafts that I'm too embarrassed to repeat.

"A new magic, yes. A magic of…forgetting."

"What do you propose?" asked a particularly wizened-looking evil wizard, who liked to remind the others how old he was and was therefore wiser than all the others. But all the other evil wizards knew that "old" doesn't mean "wise," so they usually ignored him.

Their host smiled wickedly, so broadly that his perfect teeth, whitened with the tears of innocents, blinded a few of them.

"We will enchant them, so that they forget they are slaves."

The wedding-cake wizard, Anadora, was the first to speak. "We can't do that! How will they ever know how powerful we are?"

"Oh, they'll know," said the host. "Because they will see us and our strong towers and powerful wands and fear us."

Innilji of the Horrid Breath shook his head. "But they already fear us. How will they know that we are better than them?"

"Oh, they'll know," said the host. "They'll see our expensive towers and beautiful clothes and want to be like us."

Earnywayst the Vast shook his head. "But they already envy us. How will we force them to toil for us?"

"Oh–they will," said the host, smiling so widely that birds a hundred miles away began their morning song, believing the sun to have risen. "We will convince them that, if they work hard enough for us, they will become like us."

The wizards all applauded. It seemed a very, very good idea. And the idea of their slaves working very hard made them particularly happy, because there is nothing worse than a lazy slave.

But one wizard, who had not yet spoken because he was too lazy to move his lips except to eat decided that he would tell everyone what's what.

"This will not work," he said, slowly, in shallow, breathless voice. "They will see through our magic."

The applause ended, the wizards tittered, and the host leaned forward in his chair. "Do tell, oh Nallowmouth the Nayer."

The other evil wizards sighed. Nallowmouth talked very, very slowly, which made them very impatient, and waiting was against their lazy life-styles. Several wizards had specifically enslaved waiters for this very reason.

"They will know they are slaves, because their dead will tell them."

The host laughed. "No, no. Not if we they cannot hear them. We shall make it so they are deaf to them."

Nallowmouth spoke again after a few minutes, surprising everyone with his urgency.

"They will know they are slaves, because their priests will tell them."

Again, the host laughed. "No, no. We shall tempt their priests with money. Nothing shuts up the mouthpieces of the gods like the promise of coin." He'd thought of everything, and the lazy, evil wizards nodded sagely.

"But," said Nallowmouth, by now quite exhausted. "They will know they are slaves, because the stars and animals and forests, who do not toil and do not have masters–they will tell them."

"Nallowmouth the Nayer, you tire me with your naysaying! We will convince them the forests and the animals do not talk, and that the stars are just balls of fire. We will make them think the animals are only for food and the forests are only for wood and the very soft paper they clean our butts with, and we will give them celebrities."

But Nallowmouth was not done, though he looked about to pass out from the effort of talking.

"They will know they are slaves!" he almost shouted, "because the land beneath them will always tell them the truth, and the witches of the land will not shut up."

This time, the host did not laugh. A cold wind blew in from one of the high, narrow windows, and because being lazy gives one poor circulation and they were too lazy to close the window, the wizards shivered terribly.

They sat this way for some time, depressed.

The slaves would all come for them and throw them from their towers like they'd done to Gurdlebuff the Greasy and nothing could stop them. Their slaves might even stop cleaning their butts for them after they shat.

But just as they were all about to become very sad and give up, the host understood what must be done.

"Then we will make them believe there is no magic."

The wizards gasped. No more dangerous spell was there than making people forget about magic.

"We will convince witches that magic is only about feeling good, like what we did with Yoga. And if they hear the land speak, they will think they are going crazy. And if the land tells them they should revolt, they will say that sounds uncomfortable and they will hold workshops on crystal-healing and write books on getting in touch with their spirit animals. And when they no long believe in magic, they will build supermarkets and amusement parks and watch television."

"Oooh," said the wedding-cake wizard, Anadora. "I want to go to an amusement telemarket!"

And this time Nallowmouth had nothing to nay.

So the wizards held a vote, because they believed in Democracy. And they voted the way evil wizards vote, with a ballot box and flashy election advertisements and campaign promises, and then threw out all the ballots and declared a winner because it was Democracy.

And they all voted to disenchant the world, and to make their slaves think they were free.

And they cast their spells and left their towers and went on to rule the world lazily ever after.

But it is said, in secret whispers in old forests, that the spell did not quite work the way they'd hoped.

Though everyone began to think they were free instead of slaves, some still felt like slaves.

Though the priests all were tempted with nice houses and fast cars, some still remembered to listen to gods.

Though great factories rose to turn the forests into butt-paper, some forests still whispered, and were heard.

And though witches held workshops on inner-peace and crystals, some still gathered poisoned roots from the remembering land, and plotted.

And the evil wizards? The spell was a bit too powerful, perhaps, and they too were disenchanted. They put away their robes for business suits, their towers for mansions, and their wands for fast cars.

But they are still there, and they are still the masters, and we are all still, for a little while longer, their slaves.

The Forest
That
Will Be

Love Notes From The Abyss, IV

There is no time for Love, because there is no time in Love.
Love is what time strives to become,
before and after.

The Jetz-zeit is the moment of Love,
which is every moment,
and none.

There is no opposite of Love,
only all the time before
and all the time after.

You fear the future, you desire the past.
You desire the future, you fear the past.
And what is birthed between them?

"Dread is desire for what you fear," said the existentialist, but he looked only one way.
Dread is also fear for what you desire.

The Forest That Will Be

Two powers, bright, heavy, warp the Abyss around them,
twins birthed from the moment of Love,
birthed into the moment before Love.

They pull, they desire.
The push, they fear.

Towards each other,
then flung way,
pulled back.
They fuck,
they fight.

Which is the dark, which is the light?
Not what you think.

Fear is the light, not the dark.
We light torches and candles and lamps against what we fear, to make it
flee, to see what we cannot know.

Desire is the dark, not the light.
In shadow do things become touched, the crash in the darkened bedroom
between two bodies, the stubbed toe against chair, the outreached hand towards the unseen familiar, the grasped cock and breast to bring the other
closer.

You dread when you cannot desire more than you fear, running from what
you've seen.
You dread when you cannot fear more than you desire, fleeing towards the
thing approaching.

In your Abyss are two stars, within and without.
If they do not crash in their racing,
if they do not accelerate away in their repulsion,
they are caught,
orbiting,
unable to flee,
unable to become one.

But they do not orbit each other,
but around a third they birth together.

And from this springs the eternal moment,
the now moment,
the still-point
the Jetz-zeit,
before and after time,
the fire of creation,
the serpent and the crow
becoming one.

And from this is birthed the world.

Awaiting Night's Final Falling

[fragment]

In the forest house are the gathered, the friends, the mystics; speeches, falling leaves, acclaim and dread, waiting whispers, tearful meetings and farewells. Some great intersection, a conclave at a crossroads in a pillared cathedral of towering trees.

Smoke rising from far-off conflagrations makes the hearth-fire around which we sit seem profane under darkening bower, the light-giving lanterns a sorrowful glow in the gloam of the day.

And I am there, but I am also elsewhere, looking always towards him, catching his glance, awaiting the moment of silence and what comes after.

In all the clamor I await night's final falling, when my words are no longer for others but only for him—that moment, before settling slumber, when tongue and lip have no other demand, but may finally trace the contour of muscle below the fur of his chest.

All That Is Without You

The gods are madness, and so is love.

I couldn't sleep for the noise; her wails clawing deep into my brain more fiercely when I'd close my eyes. In waking distraction, I could shut her out a little—loud music, pointless conversation, anything to drown out her pain. But in bed next to my lover, her pain was intolerable, becoming pain so loud it became my pain, and I couldn't make her shut up.

I tried drinking. It doesn't take much to get me drunk, a beer, maybe two. And I could pass out a bit, let the world spin behind my eyelids, except then, even there in that membranous darkness, she was there. Worse—she wasn't alone.

My lover said that he couldn't hear her, but he'd wake from dreams shaking. "I saw something in the room last night," he said. Fleshy, like a small man, but not human.

"In a dream?" I asked.

"Uh…sort of. I mean, I think I was awake. I was gonna wake you, but then I went back to sleep."

I showered, dressed, went to work, said nothing else. At least at work, I couldn't hear her. At least at work, I wasn't the "crazy" one. I had a client tell me a bedbug climbed into her vagina and impregnated her with a Pleiadian Ascended Master. She was crazy. I? I was just going mad.

The difference? My clients can't stop the voices from coming.
I can.
I can make them stop, but that's worse than death.
Love is madness, and so is the Other.
You can shut those voices off, close them off.
I remember it well, the day I closed them out.
Close my eyes, and it's there: the white tower, the ravens flying about them, a pillar of light from a twinned moon. She looks at herself from above into below; she looks back. And there's the tower, and there are the ravens. And I can't take it any longer.

Besides, I was in love, and how could he understand? How could any understand? How could anyone?

I wrote in my journal, "I don't want to see these anymore." No more tower; no more bones behind the tower; no more whispers; no more trembling power.

And it stopped.

Nothing. Silence, like the grave. I'd go to work; listen to tales of ancient lizard men and psychotronic silver disks, about the machine under the university which, like St. Anthony, helped homeless people find lost things and also urinate themselves.

And I was safe. Safe from them, safe from the Other, safe in an other.

You can hide there for a little while, just like you can hide in work, or hide in drugs. You can even hide in madness, at least for a little while.

Until they come back.

We do not have time for the Other, we do not have time for Love

A few years later, I'm trying to sleep, fearing again the dreams peopled by characters I know too well—and fear.

The woman with the dark iron vat won't let me pass, but I can't go back through the town whose streets were so full of those with power, those with power-over, those I must flee.

But the Other does not let you pass until you answer the unasked question.

You cannot hide from the Other. The Other chases you, hunts you. You can flee the dreams of sleeping; flee into waking for a little while. But then they chase you there.

And so you flee into sleep. You flee in waking, and like that chase of Ceridwen, after the awen-thief. You cannot stop until you are consumed and, too, become The Other.

The Other is all that is without you, and all that is within.

Love is the madness of the Other, the Other is the madness of Love

The voices continue, but you can shut them out. And I remember how a friend shut them out.

She'd been joking one day, a decade ago, flirting, and touched my finger. "I'm giving you a wart," she says, fingernail touching index above the knuckle.

"Why would you say that?" I'd asked, appalled.

"I don't know," she shrugged, looking confused herself.

And I showed her the hand a month later, benign annoying growth, rough, ugly. Then her face pale, her voice cold, she shook her head. "What the? I didn't?"

"You said," I said, feeling her terror.

"That's—that's just weird. I didn't really make that happen, did I?"

And I didn't know how to reassure her, and she didn't know how to take it back. She became angry. Wouldn't talk about it. It didn't happen, it didn't happen, stop pretending, you're making this up, I didn't do it.

"But you said…" I said, worried, upset.

And finally. "Okay, I did. I don't want to talk about it, okay? I'm sure there's some explanation. I don't want to talk about it."

We hadn't talked for a decade. A decade later I see her, after seeing standing stones and gods, after druid mountains and visions. She'd never spoken of it again. In a cafe, she and I. Would she believe what I'd seen, or deride all I'd been? I'd tell her anyway, though the tale would be tough.

But she spoke first, fearful. "I hear voices, Rhyd. Not like I'm crazy … but more—I cry. I can hear all the sorrow of people sleeping, and I can hear their voices, and I turn up music to make it stop."

Her magic radiating like silver, tinged with fear, and I laugh, tell her my tale.

"So you understand?" she said, only half asking.

"I think I do," answering, and then "remember that wart?" showing her where it'd once been.

And she shrugged, smiling. "That was weird, huh?"

Love is the Other. The Other is Love.

I'd shut them out, like she'd shut out that power.

You can shut them out, the terrors, all the illuminating fears. The Other whispers, but you can talk over this. The Other speaks, but you can shout them out. Sometimes, even the Other shouts but, by then, you can't silence them without drugs.

Or you can, because there's always an other to which you can run, someplace safe, someone in which to hide, and the Other will eventually fall silent. But when you do this you have not won, but have very much lost.

The Other is like Love, and just as terrifying.

What are we afraid of?

The Other is not myself; the other is not me.

And suddenly, you are not all there is; you are not one; you are not complete. You are you, and there is an other. And no longer are you complete, no longer are you one. You are broken, divided between self and World, sundered ground broken open to make room for something both self and Other.

Meet him and you are terrified, and you call this desire, you call this love. Hear her voice, and you are missing, empty; though you thought you'd been full.

And suddenly every song reminds you of them. On the street, a woman shakes her head, hair cascading for a moment in sunlight like the way you saw her hair once do. And that woman is her, but that woman is not her, and you are broken, and you are happy. You were everything before her, now you are nothing until she is near you again.

Meet him and you cannot breathe except when he is there holding you, though your lungs have never once failed. You are strong, but suddenly weak unless you see his smile, and also weak when you see his grin, and nothing is ever the same.

Love and the Other are indivisible by one.

Love of an other, or others, reminds you are sundered, infinity no longer divisible by one.

And just the same, the Other.

See a crow feather at your feet and hear a god, an angle of sunlight and see another. Hear winds through branches; there's a third, embers in a hearth and yet another Other.

The moon is no longer just the moon, but also every goddess of her face. But the moon is also just the moon, but no longer alone, no longer just itself, just as you are no longer just yourself in love.

And to see the Other, to fall in love, you need only surrender to the endlessness of being.

I remember when I saw the tower again, because I no longer wanted to unsee the tower.

I remember when I saw the moon again, because the moon would not stop being seen.

I work with the mentally-ill, those who hear the voices and cannot shut them out like us. And they are told that they are sick; they are told that they are unwell, and they are given what we can give to help quell that sundered pain.

And I try not to admit what I see when they are staring, shouting at a corner at a voice inside their head. I try not to look there, where they are looking, because I do not want to admit, I do not want to say, I do not want to allow that I see their Other too.

A client shouts at a demon in a corner, and I see the lingering spirit and shrug, unable to help.

A client predicts the birth of my friend's twins, and we shake our heads, pretending what we didn't hear.

A client medicalised for talking to rocks and trees, and I try not to think on him as I lay under Alder by granite, hearing them talk back.

The Other's all that is without us, and all that is within,
And what are we doing, shutting them out?
We're being good workers, we're being good slaves.
Stand in ritual; call a god; wipe them off and tuck them away when you're done, when it's time to go home to the television and kids because the weekend's over and you've got to make a living.
Fall in love and call in sick, but love can only be love 'till the rent and cable's due.
It's easier to be alone, cut off, shut down. Close them out, the other and The Other, and though without meaning, everything is safe.
The gods linger, the other waits, the madness beckons.
The Other is madness, and so is love.
And we are never alone.

If You'll Not
Die Antinous

How could I not be grateful
to her, the Lady Maple who
with branches windowed silver
framed her lover the moon, in
distant light and darkened leaf
became wild thoughts of you–

Or to the stars, just later, a Wheel,
just before eyes looked downward,
saw forlorn flower and concrete shore
while all this time your presence
breathed from light to love
across vast oceans and air?

If you'll not die Antinous
I'll tear down emperors' walls, but still
with monuments of words, build poems
to gods whose shifting faces
look also now like yours.

Fire in Winter

You remind me
Of someone I've never met.
I know this ache,
what all is taken
from what I feared
would not last a winter
Here's wood, stacked, next to
words, leaves of books
I'd been saving
for a longer winter, one
where ground and where stone
heave ice-drowned rivers
stagnant glassed ponds
breathing white sun.
You've reminded me
Of someone I've met
Yet not, yet felt
in aches in hollows
carved by unseen hands

The Forest That Will Be

in slumber of winter.
Here's sap, leaking, from
cone, limb and cock
pitched resin, gathered
for last winter's hearth.
You are familiar, kin
of Someone I've met
and remember, His
ache, hollowed echo
in ice-rimed caverns
where dreams sleep in winter.
You satyr, wooden
You dryad en-fleshed
I'm covered in pitch
Smelling of winter
and sulphur, this match
and what comes after.

Putting Out

Early in the summer of 2009, I whiled a fantastic summer with a lover in a beautiful apartment in Kreuzberg, Berlin. In the mornings (or what passes for morning in a city where Capitalism has not fully conquered the human day), we'd stumble down a short flight of steps into a scene of wonder—into a stone courtyard, out through the heavy wooden gate on the cobbled sidewalk, grapevines and trees and street art soaking my senses in luxurious intensity.

From there, one could walk to the tree-lined canal, the enchanting and very crowded outdoor Turkish Market, along a bustling street filled with food-shops and stores. Or cross a bridge to one of the nearby 15 gay bars (a fraction of the full number in that city), or descend underground to the U-bahn and travel briefly to anywhere else in that gorgeous, intoxicating city.

He was there to do research for his master's thesis on queer occult societies during the Weimar Republic, a period of unrivaled gay and Pagan culture in the period just before the Nazis rose to power. Set powerfully into the collective memory by the writings of Christopher Isherwood and the musical Cabaret, Weimar Berlin was a fascinating mix of radicalism and sexual experimentation in the midst of a breakdown of Capitalist power.

People were poor but sexy, and Berlin became both a pilgrimage site for queers in the Western world as well as a 'degenerate' symbol of all that was wrong with the world for the rising Nazi party.

Berlin had a church attendance rate of 1 , hosted occult events nightly, and the literature and art from that time speaks to an almost utopic exploration of the human soul. Oh, and it was also full of prostitutes, but we'll get to that in a bit.

I've never made much money, never much more than minimum wage. Thing is, Berlin is cheap, or was when we first stayed there. One of the ways to keep your costs down when traveling is to find an apartment to sublet. Costs of food go down significantly when you've access to a kitchen, and generally the cost of renting someone else's home is usually much lower than a nightly hotel.

To do this, I searched a few free listing sites on the internet. There was no AirBnB or other "services" yet, but sites like Craiglist.org existed where people could list for free. Each time I stayed in Berlin, the cost of renting an entire apartment (including the aforementioned one) was a little less than 100 euro (110 us dollars at the time) per week. As a matter of fact, in each instance, I rented someone else's home for the exact cost that they incurred for rent on their place.

One time we asked the person from whom we rented why they weren't charging us more. Their answer was quite shocking, and they sounded awfully offended. They'd said: "I'm not trying to make a profit here! What sort of person would do that?

While I'm near 40 years old now, this is a good time to tell you that I'm not engaging in nostalgia for an economy that existed several decades ago. This was only 5 years ago.

Kapital Über Alles

Things have changed there, as they have also changed here, on account of a shift of social relations described by cheerleaders of Capitalism as "The Sharing Economy."

On the face of it, AirBnB, a company which offers to set up people looking for sublets with hosts for a fee, appears to have made it easier to find lodging at a cheaper rate than hotels. However, it has actually all but displaced the older model which enabled someone poor like myself to stay in a foreign city.

The advent of businesses such as AirBnB, Uber, Lyft, Taskrabbit, and many other services are all part of this brave new economic world, where people can sell or rent their services to strangers at a piece-rate in return for money. The enthusiasm for these corporations and their apps is intense, soaked in the usual optimism any new capitalist venture generates through the capitalist media.

It may seem almost a sort of liberation. If you own a car, you now have the option to make money from it. If you're in need of extra cash, you can turn extra hours into waged-labor by running errands through Taskrabbit or Postmates. And on the off-chance you've got an empty room in your home, have an extra home, or have the option to stay elsewhere, you can rent out your place to others for more money than you pay in mortgage or rent. It's a brave new world, full of opportunities to make money at every turn, the possibility of liberation from the drudgery of the old ways breathing down your neck before us.

Except, it's not new. And it's not liberating.

To understand this matter, we need first to deconstruct and discard the ridiculous description of this activity as "the Sharing Economy."

Let's take the first part, "Sharing." What precisely is being 'shared' when a driver signs up with a company like Uber? Uber's not doing any sharing—in fact, Uber provides nothing to a driver except for access to their application system which provides drivers with customers. According to Uber's VP of operations:

> Uber currently keeps 20 of each trip as a lead gen cost. This percentage is common in the industry and commonly referred to as a farm out fee. There are no monthly fees to be a driver on Uber, outside of a minimal data charge for the iPhone.

Does "farm out" sound familiar at all? If you remember anything about the early history of Capitalism, you may be familiar with "Putting Out," the system by which merchants distributed raw materials to individuals in homes to assemble products (textiles, pins, matches, etc.) Farming out is a similar process, a loaning-out of access to resources in return for a high percentage of profits or income.

Uber, AirBnB, and all the other players in The Sharing Economy are not actually sharing at all, they're "putting out" access to customers.

Likewise, though, those who are using these services to make money from their homes or cars are not "sharing" either, unless sharing no longer means what we were taught it meant in kindergarten. I was told it meant letting someone use something you weren't using, and I don't remember a monetary exchange.

Let's be clear. Charging money to allow someone to use something of yours is not called sharing. It's called renting.

The Means of (Re)Production

When I first moved to Seattle, I was mostly homeless. 23, gay, new to a city, with only two friends to rely upon who lived in a suburb. To find a place, I needed money, and to find money, I needed a job, and all the jobs were in the city, not the suburb.

I slept rough many nights in those first few months. Sometimes on a stranger's couch, sometimes in an alley, often in a park, once in a while in a friend's car. More often than not, though, I'd find myself trading sex for a place to sleep.

I'm hardly ashamed. I found myself in some fantastic condos with great views, waking in the morning occasionally even to breakfast and once to a marriage proposal. It was a way to survive, most of the men were polite, and it was usually consensual except for the whole "you have a roof, I don't" bit.

It's called sex-work. And it's a common means of survival for the poor, particularly when they have no access to the things you require to survive.

"Things you require to survive," by the way, is called the Means of Reproduction in Marxist theory. This includes food, housing, and leisure—the stuff that keeps you alive.

The Means of Production is slightly different—it's access to the ability to create things others find socially useful, like cooking, art, coding…pretty much anything that we call "work." In capitalist countries, most people don't have the Means of Production and have to rely on the rich for ways to do things others will want to trade for.

The one thing a human always has, by the way, is their body. Though not all sex-workers do so from extreme poverty—and some of the greatest, most creative and powerful folks I know are sex-workers—the body is the one thing we can always fall back upon when we have nothing else.

In fact, that's what all waged-work is—our bodies being used in exchange for money. The sex-worker is no different from the tech worker, except one's a lot more likely to be beaten, raped, or vilified than the other, and, also, one's more likely to be a woman.

My Means of Production as a homeless person happened also to be my Means of Reproduction, as sex is a social relationship and part of the ways in which we create meaning in our lives. In the best scenarios, sex is a freely-given exchange between two or more people; in patriarchal marriages, or in rape, or in situations of economic disparity, that exchange is not freely-given.

But this is the same with that category of social-relations called labor, too. I only work for someone richer than myself because they have money and I do not. While I have some choice in whom I work for (just as I had some choice in who I let fuck me when I was homeless), it's difficult to say that I was fully able to exercise my free will. We who have no wealth must work to survive in a Capitalist society because the laws ensure we have no other choice.

We are always trading our Means of Reproduction (again, the very essence of our life) for access to the Means of Production. We sell our body (whether that be our mental faculties, our social skills, our muscles, or our genitals) in exchange for money we use to purchase what will give us the life we can get, to feed our Reproduction.

Pimp My Life

When I traded sex for a place to stay for the night, there was no one else directly mediating that exchange. Guy takes a homeless guy back to his place, homeless guy gets a place to sleep, housed guy gets sex with someone younger than him, and that's the end of the transaction.

But…what if there were some enterprising person eager to get in on this social exchange? Say, some agent who helped make such connections in return for money from the buyer or oral sex from the seller?

Such folks exist, of course.

A pimp or madam offer both a steady stream of clients to a sex-worker as well as some semblance of security. The better ones keep the prostitutes they manage safe from abusive buyers, provide safer places for the sex to occur, and even screen customers beforehand. They may even help those under their employ get to the hospital or pay for contraception or treatment for sexually transmitted infections (that is, work injuries.) Basically, benefits.

Much, much more common, however, are the abuses. A pimp or madam wields great power over their sex-workers, and the litany of horrors people endure must be remembered. One of the most common is stolen wages: the person acting as the intermediary demands a cut of income from the sex-work, despite not performing any of the work themselves, justifying this extortion through their 'services' of providing protection and a steady stream of clients.

Worst of all, the sex-worker cannot easily end their relationship with the pimp or madam out of fear of violence, poverty, and losing access to customers (that is, their Means of Production).

There was no pimp to arrange these meetings between myself and the men I slept with, though I've had plenty such pimps in my life. They're called employers.

I realize, for many, my comparison between Capitalist employment and sex-work may be upsetting. For some, sex-work is always exploitative, while waged-labor is seen (particularly by those who are not convinced Capitalism is all that bad) as more respectable and free-willed.

To those of this opinion, I'll admit–it's a lot easier to talk of my time working in restaurants than it is my time trading sex. And let's be awfully honest: sex work is not highly paid. But favoring one sort of work over another is why a CEO is paid millions while an immigrant janitor's paid pennies.

And to those worried I'm ignoring my male privilege, I'll admit—I'm pretty strong and a little scary looking—my experiences were certainly less dangerous than many of my trans and non-male friends who've engaged (and currently engage) in sex-work face.

That said, we should insist that sex-work is work, just as any other work is work. And work when you have no choice is exploitative. Either all work should be legal, or all work should be illegal (I vote for the latter).

There's an App For That

So, hey…let's return to that Sharing Economy thing, huh?

I guess you could kinda say that I was "sharing" my body with those men. On the better nights, with the more attractive and fascinating and kind men, it did kinda feel like sharing, except, well–no. I was renting myself to them.

Again, I was turning my Means of Reproduction into something I could trade so I could get what I needed, which is the deal we all make with the Capitalists.

This Sharing Economy shit is a really pretty name we put on people renting out their life in exchange for money, turning their cars and homes into the Means of Production. And we must be really clear about what AirBnB, Uber, and all these companies really are.

They're pimps. They're extracting money from social transactions we make with each other.

When you need a ride from a friend, you offer to pay them gas money. Now, you pay Uber who pays the driver less than what you paid, while the driver bears all the responsibility (insurance, car payments, gas, repairs).

A Kindness of Ravens

When you're going to be gone from your home for a few weeks, you might ask a friend to house-sit or even offer to let a stranger stay if they pay your rent while you're gone. Now, AirBnb gets to make money off of you doing so.

What gushing white tech CEO's and their slobbering fan-boys declare is a "new economy" is really just another way to extract money from the most basic of human activities, a new Enclosure of the social Commons.

Capitalism in Crisis

There's that quote about remembering history, that I won't repeat here. Better to say this: certain forms repeat throughout history, and recognizing when they recur is a great way of learning to fight them. The "open-plan office" that many tech-workers rightfully complain about bears a strong resemblance to the factory floor of the 19th century, and though working for Google is nothing like working in a sweat-shop, noticing the similarities helps remind us when the powerful are relying on something that's worked for them in the past.

Our current society is not really like Weimar Berlin just before the Nazis rose to power, mostly because what passes for art and culture and sexual experimentation is rather mundane and banal compared to what they came up with. Nor is using Uber or renting out your apartment with AirBnB quite like the putting-out industry of 1700's England. And selling your sex is not the same as using TaskRabbit.

But the forms repeat. In Berlin, the weakness of Capitalism compelled people to rent their bodies for money. In early 1700's England, greedy people "put-out" resources to have the poor make money for them. And really awful people have always tried to get a piece of us, whether it be our sex or any of the other social relations we create.

Capitalism is in another crisis. It does this, repeatedly, and in those moments where the rich aren't certain they'll be able to hold onto their wealth, they turn all their attention towards finding new ways of extracting our Means of Reproduction and turning it into their profit.

You're being pimped.

What are you gonna do about it?

Tears In An Other World

In An Other world, we will gather the tears of those who cry in love, sitting at night on doorsteps, alone.

Each tear fallen caught in fairy-cups, glistening in Ceridwen's moonlight, will be the most sought-after draught, saline drops of distilled desire falling from eyes whose attempts to love have seen the fear of loss.

They do not need them, these tears. They are what is left over, what spills out when so much love can no longer be held inside the soul.

In An Other world, there will be no such thing as too-much love, because it will be gathered, held close in tiny teacups born in even smaller hands, carried as gifts to those who do not have enough love. To children without parents, to widows whose bodies have long been untouched by the sweating palms of lusting lovers, to those who have lost, to those who have never been loved.

But there will be no unloved in An Other world, for the poets and dreamers who cry at night upon doorsteps, their tears glistening in Ceridwen's moon, have more than enough love to give the world.

The Multitude &
The Myriad

The sun is not the brightest star, but it is the closest, the loudest. The sun is so close that it blinds from our eyes all those others who, by mere virtue of distance, must wait for the darkest of hours to remind us of their light. Without that garish ferocity, we cannot live, but it is at the cost of the myriad that this one Truth shines upon us.

If these words were in German, her warmth could bronze and perhaps sear your skin with rays of feminine brilliance. Were you reading this in French, his beckoning light might bring you instead to think on his mannish illumination gently coaxing out the life of plant from soil. The sun is feminine in many Germanic languages, while masculine in many Latin-derived tongues, and the moon is likewise gendered. It is female in French and male in German.

Is the sun male or female, though? It certainly cannot be said to have identifiable genitalia, so we are unable to resort to a particularly base methodology to discover our answer. One might even suggest that it has no gender at all, in accordance to our manner of ordering nouns in English. If this is the case, though, we must immediately judge all speakers of languages which gender the sun to be fools or, charitably, inheritors of a hopelessly primitive linguistic system.

Another interesting possibility exists. Perhaps the sun is both female and male, according to how and where one views it. We know, certainly, that the sun can both give life and take life away. It can both warm and burn; it might illuminate or blind depending upon where you happen to be standing or looking. That is, the sun is many things simultaneously; many things to many people. In the far northern hemisphere, I experience it in subtle degrees as the year grows cold. My friends in that other hemisphere now feel its coming strength as their winter thaws and spring flowers bloom. Those betwixt our homes at this moment shield their eyes from it, sweating fiercely under its burdensome weight.

The sun is both warm and cold, distant and close, searing and life-giving. Within Her and His and Its intensity is all the contradictions and opposites which compose a wholeness, a unity only understood in its fragmented difference.

One, Two, None, All

For more than a millennium there was one God. Before, there were many, but then there was but one, and he was male—a fierce, strong, creator-lord full of justice and power, might and judgment, as well as love, mercy, and some degree of kindness to those deserving of his favors or loyal to his causes.

We need not be so simple about it, though. There were certainly others gods; otherwise our Paganism is mere aesthetic, and vast civilizations utterly misguided, as the fundamentalist believers in Progress would have us think. The "progression" of religion from Animistic Shamanism to Polytheism, then to Henotheism, then to Monotheism and finally, at the top of glorious and final present, Atheism, relies upon the hope that our present existence is somehow "better" than yesteryear.

We should consider the succession of this forced march closely. It proposes first a "simplistic" relationality between nature and humanity, followed by an unfortunate anthropomorphization of natural forces into human-gods. Then the desert cults, laboring under the searing, garish and very-loud sun, chose just one of the many and, when a prophet is hanged upon wood, they decide their one is an only. Nearly two millennia later, some French and English writers decide there's no god at all, and we are finally now enlightened. From all, to many, to one, to none–and too bad the billions in Africa and Asia just can't catch up.

Beyond the extreme arrogance of asserting that a mere 2 of the world has accurately answered the question of the existence of gods, we should specifically complicate the "evolutionary" narrative of progressive ascension. Since so many ancient and indigenous cultures think in circles and wheels rather than vertical lines, it's surprising that such a theory of religious succession could still maintain a grip upon Pagan thought . This can be seen particularly in an unfortunate misstep of Wicca regarding the gender of the gods.

A popular reading of the re-introduction of "The Goddess" into modern religious thought (not just Pagan, but also some strands of Christian Theology) is that it's a necessary correction of two millennia of male-centered, Monotheistic thought. This is a fair reading, and one can certainly point to all sorts of social and religious tendencies which, through a belief in an male-gendered Only-god, contributed to the systematic degradation of a full half of humanity. That there was only one god, and that this only-god was male, is certainly peculiar and suspicious, particularly considering the patriarchal succession of priesthoods of this only-(male)-god.

As a political act, the insistence on an equally-important Goddess was quite radical, but also incredibly problematic. Besides the failed attempts of some writers to re-narrate a matriarchal past into pre-Monotheistic Europe (and history is only narration, so we should applaud their attempts as much as we cringe at their failure), the question of the only-(male)-god is hardly answered by giving him a mate, as if the Hebrew god's act in Eden were a model to emulate.

Worse, this Goddess is a no-one; just as the monotheistic God was also a no-one. They are not just no-ones, but also All-Ones, or Half-Ones. The Pagan (particularly Wiccan) Goddess is a conglomerate principle, a pastiche, a compound being encompassing half of a split divinity gendered female, or a corporate entity sometimes named the Divine Feminine. What then is left which is not of the one-Half-(female)-Goddess is then re-pasted upon a feral-yet-civil hunter dressed up in sacred loin-cloth and antlers. And, we are thus supposed to sigh, relieved that the One-God's rib forms his eternal companion.

I do not say here that there is no Goddess, rather that there are many of them, a multitude, a myriad. Nor would it do much good for us to debate precisely the theological import of such statements like, "I acknowledge the Goddess in all Her forms" (a sort of universalist-monism) or "I worship the Goddess by her many names" (a less corporatist approach). Rather, we should ask precisely why, as inheritors and escapees of monotheistic power, we'd settle for two gods as a solution to the tyranny of the (male) one.

Being a believer in the existence of gods (by which I also mean goddessess—let none say English does not possess gender!) requires me to be a bit extra polite when another Pagan, in ritual or in conversation, speaks of Pagans collectively worshiping "The Goddess." I must do a bit of translation of their statement in order to not be offended. It's an allowance for their shorthand, regardless of how much I really wish to ask, "wait–which goddess? I've met five of them, and have heard of another eighty, at least."

To say they are all-one, that all the goddesses enfold into one great Goddess is a bit colonialist. It's also understandable, since we do the same thing with gender. We speak of "female" and "male" as if all humanity is easily divided into two sorts of people, each composing a half of a corporate whole called "humanity."

It's a short-hand, a quick-sorting category, which is certainly useful in some circumstances, but it is also only that. And, like all categories and labels, often times they don't fit, no matter how hard we try to peg certain beings into the spaces we've created for them.

Which Man? Which Woman?

Like race, we often approach the idea of gender as if it is a naturally-derived or divinely-revealed thing, though we forget we must actually be taught these categories. I had many black friends and female friends and even a few (but very few) wealthy friends when I was a child. But it was not until our differences were explained (and re-iterated, and enforced) that I understood that there was a difference between them and I. The skin-color of my friends was a mere characteristic, not a difference until I was told that being "white" meant something and being "black" meant something else. Similarly with female: a girl was a sort of a friend, not an opposition to boy. Different genitals was like different hair-length–utterly inconsequential.

But male and female, like white and black, mean something, or mean something to lots of people. Being one means you get paid less, being the other means you get paid more. It's better to be white and male than all the other things, depending on where you live, but only because people have decided that white and male are better things than black or female.

Even our divine was male for awhile (and maybe even white, judging from most popular depictions of Jesus). Having a female divine as well is certainly nice and having her be equal (and in some traditions superior) to him corrects some imbalances certainly.

But there are many sorts of men, and many sorts of women. There are very old, withered-but-wise men, and very young, mewling, just-out-of-the-womb men. There are the strong and muscled ones, the furry ones (my favorite), but also the lithe or round ones. And the same for women: the maidens, the mothers, the crones, the really strong ones and the really graceful ones, the large and fecund or the diminutive and fierce. To say they are all women or are all men is a strange thing to say.

There are several ways people have gone about re-imagining gender, or re-enforcing gender, and these attempts are worth staring at.

One of perhaps the more common treatments has been to re-inforce the divisions between them, cutting deeper "no-man's lands" betwixt her and him. One strand of thought focuses primarily on the genitals of the person, and to some degree the genetics. On the side of "her" has been Z Budapest and other Second-Wave feminists, insisting that women are only those who've been born into such things as "the uterine mysteries."

On the side of "him" have been writers characteristic of the New Right gaining increasing popularity within Paganism, such as Jack Donovan. "Men" for them are those who possess not just testicles, but also certain physical characteristics defined precisely by their opposition to an imagined Feminine.

In both cases, it is the fault of the other which has brought them to such matters. Second-Wave feminists cite patriarchy as the cause of their need for exclusion, and writers like Donovan cite Feminism as the reason men are bound to desk-work and served "manly" drinks in thin stemware.

A second treatment of gender fails equally. The "Radical Feminism" (which is hardly radical at all) of people like Lierre Keith and Derrick Jenson of Deep Green Resistance, as well as certain positions leftover from late 60's American Paganism, attempts to resolve the matter of gender by abolishing it altogether. On its surface, such an idea is appealing, as must have been Atheism to Enlightenment writers, noting the problems of European Monotheism. Without gender, there is no division, and all humanity becomes one. Only in its particular violence against a certain group of people, however, does one begin to see the flaws in this.

In fact, what all these attempts have in common is a shared hatred of a specific class of people–trans-folk. Humans, who have chosen to physically embody a gender according to their will rather than circumstance of birth, attract such vitriol from all these groups that we should seriously consider why. Donovan, Budapest and Keith, all on apparently opposite sides of the gender question, stand united in their venom against trans-folk. Why?

The trans-person (and, equally perhaps, the queer) stands in a place more revolutionary and radical than any of their critics can hope to occupy.

By choosing their gender, they do not abolish gender, they transform it into a human act, reminding the rest of us that gender, like race, is something we create and can choose to embody, rather than something we are born into. The all is split into many; each half of humanity split into a multitude of individual embodiments.

This transformation is revolutionary because it affects the rest of us. I am a cis-male, deep voiced, muscular, "man," but if I rely only on accident of birth to claim my specific maleness, I exist in a passive realm of non-choice. For the multitude of other sorts of men, is it not the same thing? As well, for women; if a female relies on her uterus for her identity, what sort of identity is that?

That is, we cannot merely say woman, we must also ask "which woman?" Just as we cannot merely say Goddess or God, but rather ask which goddess? Which god?

The Multitude and the Myriad

To lump a very large group of things, or people, or beings into one whole has not gone very well for us humans these past few millenia, particularly because we've had to, like Cinderella's step-sisters, take some bloody steps to force things to fit into the receptacle of our categories.

Monotheism required the annihilation of other gods except the One God; just as it required the destruction of cultural forms to make people fit into its categories. Authoritarian Communism and Fascism both require similar annihilation, crushing all humans within their realm into the worker or the volk. But likewise, Atheism is hardly an adequate answer, which abolishes all gods just as some would abolish all gender. More pernicious has been Capitalism's answer, which erases identity altogether, except what can be purchased or sold, leaving individuality to one's choice of smartphone or automobile. Any anyway, it hates forests.

Antonio Negri and Michael Hardt introduced the idea of "the Multitude," the vast teeming flood of humans and their experiences which threaten always to overwhelm Empire. I suggest we Pagans embrace it and expand upon it. I like, particularly, the word Myriad, as in a "myriad of stars," an immeasurable number which likely has a limit but one we cannot quite reach.

A Kindness of Ravens

In all our multitudes of experience, we define ourselves and our genders. Each man is a sort of man, each woman a sort of woman. Each goddess is a sort of goddess, each god a sort of god. They are themselves them selves, just as we are each neither cog nor component.

How many gods are there? I do not know, anymore than I could hope to innumerate the sorts of women I've met, or of trees. I know it's more than two and, definitely, more than none.

Likewise, how many ways of encountering the Other, or of making love, or of relating to each other are there? How many sorts of sunlight are there, how many kinds of illumination does the sun shine upon the earth?

A multitude, certainly.

A Myriad.

What Do They Mean?

"I think I need to tell you something."

I'm trying not to scowl at the man who's interrupting me again. It's Lugnasadh, two years ago, a warm sun pouring through the willow branches onto my ruined circle.

I'm still grumpy with him. Today's the first time I braved a public druid ritual to honor the wheel of the year, sitting in a park along Lake Washington in a small grove not far from the ruins of a highway on-ramp. I'm in an area not often frequented by most people except a certain sort of people, but I thought I was far enough away from their recreation to remain unbothered.

Besides I look dour, and I'm sitting with lit incense surrounded by feathers and stones, a grizzled man with a shaved head, doing bizarre druid-things in an obscure corner of a massive park. I figured no-one would approach me.

But this guy? He walked right through my circle, clutching a book, oblivious to everything except my sudden barking, "Hey!"

I'd yelled at him. I'm not really proud of that. He was elderly, perhaps in his early 60's. And I rued my reaction even more when he returned.

A Kindness of Ravens

In my defense, though, I was sitting not very far from a gay cruising area where men—often married and officially 'straight'—would have quick, detached sex with strangers in bushes. I love the area itself: haunted, post-apocalyptic, a place where humanity's failed attempts to conquer nature still linger in ruins. I just wasn't looking for what they were looking for.

I'd chosen the place because it was far enough away from mundane folks that I'd be ignored, relying on its reputation as a sexual playground to drive middle-class white families away. But this meant I risked being inter-rupted by men suspecting I was on-display in their outdoor bazaar, and I'd occasionally notice some awkward man or other, still wearing his tie and wedding ring, tentatively approaching me before noting the lit candles and incense and steering back toward easier prey.

So when this man walked, utterly oblivious, through my circle? You can excuse my moment of rage. I figured he was trying to hit on me, ignoring all the signs I'd put out to ward them off.

I guess I should tell you something else, though. I'd just asked the gods for a guide for the mystery they were showing me. A dark bard in the un-derworld had shown me a vision of massive destruction, and I was a bit confused. What did any of that mean? I was a bit wrecked, really—I knew there was something I needed to understand, but I couldn't, and I'm sitting at the gate of Lugnasadh begging for a guide and this fucker just walks right through my circle.

Maybe you're laughing. I am, now.

"I think I need to tell you something," he said, returning to the edge of my re-cast circle after a few minutes of sitting by the water, reading. He was staring at me, or actually at the pile of crow feathers in front of me."

I relaxed my scowl. "It's okay, really," I answered. My concentration was broken; this ritual wasn't happening anyway. And then, not really knowing why, I invited him over to where I was sitting and handed him a crow feather.

I didn't expect his awe when I did this. I felt I should give him something. He was eyeing them, and I had plenty. They fall from the sky, after all, but he then started tearing up.

"Feathers—she gives me feathers. I…"

I was getting confused, but fiercely intrigued.

When he'd gathered his thoughts, he continued. "I just need to tell someone this, and now because you gave me a feather I think I needed to tell you. My wife just told me she's taking me back to an island where we first met 25 years ago. Can you believe it? I've been with her 25 years, and I didn't know I could ever be in love like this."

I wasn't in love; I hadn't been for awhile, actually, and was a bit bitter about this. Still, it was hard not to tremble in deep joy with him as he told me about her, staring at the feather in his hand.

And I don't know why I tell him this, and I don't know why he's telling me any of this, but it's all happening. And, anyway, I'd asked for a guide. "Leave that feather on the island," I suggested.

He shook his head knowingly. "I will! Thank you. Thanks for hearing my story, and again, sorry I interrupted you."

"I'm not sure you did," I said to myself, watching him walk away, dazed, happy.

What is Water?

I worship Brân, the Welsh Giant King, the Blessed Raven. With all the grand works both Odin and The Morrigan are up to, I sometimes like to remind people that there's another Raven god, but he's onto his own stuff, and it's mostly all revolution anyway.

I met Brân on an island, and in some mountains, and one time just walking down the street. I had a vision of him standing thousands of feet above a valley wearing a rippling black cloak that later proved to be millions of ravens consuming his flesh. Then, a few months later, I saw that very valley in the same storm-lit skies from the side of a mountain in France with my physical eyes.

One time, I was with a dear friend exploring an island in the middle of the Willamette river. I remember thinking of Brân the entire time that we were there and laughing when our mutual companion, noting how much difficulty we were having fording the cold river back to the shore, said "you should lay down in the water and let her cross over you."

I could go on, filling pages and perhaps books with such meaningful occurrences, what Jung called synchronicity. But more than likely, you get the point, because such things have probably happened for you, or maybe, reading this, are about to, because gods and meaning are both contagious (sorry about that—I may have just given you a flu from the Otherworld.)

Importantly, though, these events which weave a tapestry of meaning for me run generally counter to the main thrust of meaning in capitalist society.

In capitalist society, gods don't exist; just like homeless people don't really exist; just like stars are really just large balls of flaming gas. But to this I must answer, the stars are balls of flaming gas if animals are mere food and trees are mere fuel, humans mere workers and puddles mere bits of water.

That is, what something really is does not begin to describe what something means. Looking for the material being-ness of a thing, rather than its tapestry of meaning, is to destroy it. It is like disassembling a flower to know what a flower really-is, or like pulling out the veins, tendons, bones, and organs of your lover and arraying them before yourself on a table so you can learn why you love him.

That is, dissect a thing to know it and you've killed it, or at least made it no longer meaningful.

Take water. Water is made of the bonding of several atoms, atoms are tiny particles held together through poorly-understood adherence principles which can be split and reconfigured. That definitely doesn't tell us what what water actually is, let alone what water means.

Water can be in several forms, gas, liquid, solid. It dissolves things, makes other things expand. It freezes at 0 degrees Celsius (which is a measurement of heat—which is agitated particles–calibrated to that transition point of liquid water into ice), and it boils at 100 degrees Celsius.

But what's a glacier, then? What's an ice-cube? What's snow? And what's a lake, and how is it different from a river, and different from rain, or from a tropical waterfall as against the cold torrent of a northern cascade? What's a glass of water, or what's a bath, or a shower, what's the difference between steam rising from a tea-kettle or from a pot of soup or escaping from the pressure-release valve of a steam engine? What's the mist that settles on your skin as your children play in sprinklers on a summer day, and what's the mist that sprays your face on a cold day overlooking crashing waves? What's the snow falling on your tongue as you laugh with a lover, what's the snow falling on bleak streets as you wonder if your lover's car is safe on the road?

The answer to "what is water?" cannot be answered without also answering "what does water mean?"

And what water means is rarely the same to each person. The same lake where two trembling lovers declare their love to each other can be the lake where a mother goes to mourn her drowned child. What does that lake mean, then? When we ask each other the meaning of that lake, how do we determine what it 'really means' past all the varied opinions and experiences and feelings of that lake?

We have two problems here. To know a thing enough to refer to it, we must have some idea of existence outside the realm of meaning, and some way to abstract (or extract) its essence to speak about it. But by doing so, by speaking of a thing outside its meaning, we do great damage to it.

On the other hand, to know the full meaning of a thing would take more than an eternity. Who am I, really? I'm a story, not just a human—I cannot be fully known by being dissected, and every attempt to do so results in some sort of brutality against my body or meaning. Any title, any name conjured to define (de-fine, to make finite, to give ends and boundaries to) me limits my existence, closes off my meaning. I am Rhyd; I'm a gay man; I'm a queer; I'm 38; I'm a writer; I'm a poet. I'm an anarchist; I'm a lover; I'm a brother; I'm a social worker. I'm a bard and I'm a gods-worshipper. I would need an entire lifetime to define who I am with words, and this says nothing for all the meaning I have to others.

What's Meaning Mean?

But what, then, is meaning? We create meaning. Meaning is a social-act, a kind of intercourse between us and the world, and us and each other.

Let's look at Truth, briefly. What is the meaning of Truth? Truth is what something really-means or really-is, beyond all appearances or beyond all the socially-woven threads of meaning.

But what's a tapestry, really, without all the threads which weave it? It's no longer a tapestry. What are you, really, when we get to your core existence? A dead and dis-membered pile of bloody muscle and gore.

If we try to get to the Truth of a thing by reducing it, we get inert material. But if we try to get to the full truth of the thing the other direction, we face an even more impossible task, because the Truth of who I am isn't something I alone can determine. In fact, if I am the sole arbiter of the Truth of myself, that makes everything a lover has ever thought of me, or what an enemy has ever feared of me, an utter lie.

So, Truth and Meaning both exist on the same field and are mostly interchangeable, except that Truth has an opposite (falsehood), while Meaning has no opposite except its absence—Meaninglessness.

And if something is Meaningless, it means it's something we reject, we throw out, or ignore. Meaningless people do not matter to us, meaningless events become excluded from our narratives, and the very feeling of meaninglessness is what we call despair.

What does Meaning mean? What's the meaning of meaning?

These aren't just the malicious mischievous questions of a mad bard, but the very crux of our problem. Meaning can't be reduced, it only expands.

A Kindness of Ravens

Meaning has no cognate, and the only other word in the English language that comes close to functioning as its synonym is not Truth, but Love.

When I love someone, they have meaning for me. They are meaningful to me, I derive meaning from them, we mean something to each other. When I do not love someone, they hold no meaning for me; they are meaningless to me, or they mean no-thing to me.

When something means something else, or when someone means some thing, we are stating that there's a correspondence between one thing and another thing. In translation, we might ask what amour or Liebe "means" in English, which is to say "what word in my language corresponds to that word in yours?"

"Meaning" is a relational word, and there's no co-incidence that something meaningful to us is often said to give us 'reason to live.'

From the ancient philosophers, alchemists, astrologers, and magicians we have the search for the key to correspondence between one thing and another. From the modern science, we have the search for the reason for the relationship, the reckoning of something's being and existence and its correspondence to natural laws.

That is, they both search for the same key: *meaning*. Not Truth as we think of it, but Meaning. What does it mean when an organism behaves in a certain way to certain stimulae, and why does it do that? What does it mean when planets conjunct or I cast a circle and something appears, and why does it do that?

Meaning is the very key we seek, the relationship between one thing and another, the foundational drive and reasons things are what they are, and the very stuff which makes our lives livable—that is, full of meaning.

Meaning is what we actually mean when we speak of magic, and the very core of human existence. Trees don't appear to seek meaning, nor do stars or crows. And while some animists might object to the inherent anthropocentricism of such a statement, I'll say it anyway: humans are the only seekers of meaning we've yet encountered, and it's perhaps the one identifiable social contract we have both with each other and the world.

We create meaning. That's our magic, not just that of a poet or artist, but also that of a lover or a child or a friend, the sorcery both of warrior and bard, king and slave. We are meaning makers, and meaning is the thread which weaves us together.

The Jetztzeit

Walter Benjamin, a Marxist philosopher and theorist, suggested that before any revolution there's a revolutionary-moment, a time-out-of-time: the Jetztzeit (now-time). Just before that moment, all the events which would lead people to desire a revolution had occurred and seemed to rush into a single moment. The time after the Jetztzeit is an entirely new thing, all the moments stretching out from that radical still-point.

Two cards from Tarot, The Fool and The World, explain this quite well. In many depictions, The Fool is about to step off into the great unknown with only what is carried in a small bag. And in many depictions, the World is a moment of completion, an eternal moment of unity, the culmination or ending of a cycle just before a new one begins. After the World? The Fool, and after the Fool?

The Magician.

Benjamin's idea was that there are certain moments in which everything can change, in which the course of history (a narrative of meaning) can be altered, shattered, and a wholly new-thing can arise from the actions taken during that moment, the now time or Jetztzeit.

But how do you know you're in the Jetztzeit, or the revolutionary moment? It takes a certain awareness within that moment to recognize the meaning contained within that moment, the "revolutionary potential." It's the moment of the magician, the revolutionary, the poet, who acts not according to all the meaning that has existed before, but to create a new meaning in that now-time.

A man stumbles through an invisible ritual circle a moment after another man has asked for a guide. This is a Jetztzeit, a moment both meaningless yet pregnant with meaning, both the Fool and the World together. My first reaction was one of anger and frustration; I had not yet recognised the thread of meaning attached to his appearance and my request. The Jetztzeit almost disappeared, were it not for his return and my calming.

And in that moment when I recognized not what it means that the man had walked through but what it *could* mean, I performed a kind of magic, moving from The Fool to the Magician, finding a correspondence and a reckoning and a relationship between two otherwise disparate amounts.

And I use the word "recognize" here, not "understood." Because what was really The Truth of the man interrupting my ritual? There was no Truth, only potential meaning, and it was for he and I both to understand.

I needed to recognize his meaning, not just what he might mean to me, just as he recognized my meaning, not just what I might mean to him. Meaning is never a solitary act.

But sometimes others try to create our meaning for us, and to take our meaning from us.

The Poet, the Priest, the Politician

On June 17, 2015, a man named Dylan Roof sat in a prayer service of the Emmanuel African Methodist Episcopal Church, and as the people gathered, praying, he shot ten of them before escaping. Nine died.

Coming after so much recent, extreme violence against Black people in the United States, it was not hard to piece this meaningless event into the narrative of white-violence against the descendants of former slaves, particularly because the church he chose, and the victims whom he shot, were Black.

But we should remember this—the event is only itself, standing outside of meaning. It is a meaningless event until we thread meaning through it. That's not to question that narrative at all—in fact, there's an insidious war against Blackfolk in this country that has flared to new levels of horrific violence and daring.

I bring up the event as outside of meaning, however, because of one of the first narrations of the event to be broadcast by FOX news. In that segment, a conservative Black pastor is questioned regarding the event, and he states that, rather than being an attack against Blackfolk, the shooting was a clear attack on Christianity. From his viewpoint, the secular and anti-Christian sentiments in America have become so strong that people were shooting Christians in their own churches, and it was time for Christians to arm themselves to protect their religious beliefs against the infidels.

There's a lot to be said about this interview, particularly regarding the source, as FOX news is hardly known for speaking on behalf of the oppressed, unless by "oppressed" we mean white straight Christian males.

We must return here to the question of meaning and the Jetztzeit. There are certain events which stand outside the apparent 'normal' course of history, or rather outside our narratives of meaning. These events present threats to our way of understanding the world.

For a white, conservative pro-capitalist Christian heterosexual male, whose comfort and power in society (as well as his support for it) rests upon being told he is doing nothing wrong and the world is his—to such a person, a mass shooting of Blackfolk by a young white straight guy in a Christian church presents an almost violent threat to the meaning of his life and the society in which he lives.

To most of us, it's unquestionable that this shooting was part of the long history of violence against Blacks in America, even before the murderer's racist motives were revealed. But for the narrative of a post-racial secular capitalist American society, the massacre became a sort of tear in the tapestry-of-meaning that needed to be repaired—and quickly.

A much larger event from 14 years ago had a similar effect on the narratives of power. When two planes crashed into the financial center of New York City, it took days and weeks for that tear to be repaired.

Naomi Klein, in her book *The Shock Doctrine*, did significant work tying together the psychological trauma that individuals and societies suffer and the political usefulness of those traumas. Natural disasters like the flooding of New Orleans or manufactured disasters like the collapse of economies, such as what Greece is enduring now, are often sites of extreme political and economic violence, and seen by many of the powerful as a chance to re-assert a certain authority and political ideology upon people experiencing psychological, emotional, and physical traumatic shock.

What she's referring to is similar to Waltar Benjamin's Jetztzeit, as well. Disaster defies meaning, regardless of how many televangelists want to blame every hurricane and tornado on gays. Breakdowns or gaps in the normal functioning of society create similar openings in our narratives of meaning.

In those moments, what I call "traumatic gaps," there is typically some struggle to attach meaning to an event, either to pull the thing back into the main narrative of the powerful (as in the case of 9/11, or the attempt to define the Charleston shooting as an attack on Christianity), or by those who sense within the gap the way out of one world into another.

Stealing Our Meaning Back

What does it mean that gods are appearing to us? Really, what do they mean at all? I'm afraid to say, and also delighted to say, it means nothing at all, or not yet.

I'm not saying gods don't exist, otherwise attempting to rebuild the cult of Brân the Raven-King is a rather silly thing to do. Nor am I saying gods are meaningless. If anything, they are a fount of meaning itself, the patterns upon which we weave the rest of our threads of meaning.

A Kindness of Ravens

Gods aren't an ideology or a narrative. Rather, like us, they are meaning-makers. They create meaning with us, just as we create meaning with them. But as you know, we're not really supposed to believe that gods exist. Often, either we're thought crazy, or just as bad, told our experience of a goddess is actually part of some bigger Goddess. This becomes a way others attempt to steal our ability to create meaning or claim the meaning of a thing.

But why try to claim the meaning of something? The answer is precisely also why I'm an anarchist: authority and power.

We talk often of the Catholic Church and its destruction of ancient religions, but rarely do we look directly at the processes they used to do so. Beyond the sword of conquest, the pyres of the heretics, and the axes used to cut down sacred trees, there was a much more systematic theft of meaning enacted by Christians hoping to gain power over people–the Saints.

Take St. Denis, the patron saint of France. St. Denis was beheaded along with two companions when he climbed a druid-hill to evangelize them. They sacrificed him, but when his head fell off, he caught it and walked with it in his hands down the hill 6 miles to a place where he finally dropped dead. From his neck sprung vines and wine, from his head sprung a fountain.

Denis (Dennis) is the Gaulish-Latinate derivative of Dionysos, and St. Denis' martyred companion was Eleutherius. Diónysos Eleuthereús, you may know, is "Dionysos the Liberator." And the place where he was martyred? It became named "Le mont des Martres" or Montmartre, the red-light district where sex and wine flow freely, popularized for Americans by the films Moulin Rouge and Amelie. That's right. The sex-and-wine district of Paris is an ancient Druid site.

It's not hard to see why the Church might need to displace the worship of Dionysos (and the druids) in a city like Paris and claim him, embodied in a saint, as one of theirs. It helped secure their rule, especially since Dionysos The Liberator was worshiped by the underclasses and slaves.

Diónysos Eleuthereús "The Liberator" brings us back to Walter Benjamin's Jetztzeit again. An intervention or appearance of a god for us now is so unusual, so outside the apparent course of historical narrative, so 'meaningless,' that there is a rush in the moment of our experience of them to create meaning around it, to close off the traumatic gap they break open, to slam shut that gate.

As with the Jetztzeit, the moment of a god is a potential moment of liberation, even revolution, a tear in the tapestry of power around us, and a traumatic gap that others will seek quickly to close. Like the shooting in Charleston on the one hand, or the many acts of rebellion against Capitalism by Blackfolk on the other, the narratives of the powerful always try to enclose their own meaning, their own sorcery, around the Other world that we glimpse in those moments.

The meaning of our gods is currently not allowed to disrupt the main narrative of our society. It's possible one day it might, but we should also be wary of who shapes that meaning. There's already a golden bull on Wall Street, a sea-goddess on a Starbucks logo, plastic replicas of shrines to ancient gods in Disneyland and Las Vegas, and mass-produced films shaping the imagery and narratives of gods like Thor and Loki.

Perhaps our gods are not yet quite a threat to the powerful, but what this really means is that we still do not claim our meaning as our own. As long as we're happy to enjoy the safety and protection of systems-of-meaning which devalue forests and Black bodies, our gods will be our own personal secret story.

But if one day we seize the moment of the poet and the revolutionary, embrace the Jetztzeit of the gods, and seek to reclaim our own meaning, than we should certainly expect resistance.

We should be ready.

The Forest That Will Be

The Gates again open, the skies darken, the rain soaks through stone and skin.

I.

The rain poured through my skin. As I stood upon the pavement outside the tavern, soaked in the chill night, smoking a cigarette, the Gates opened around me.

Straddling the ford, wet up to the laces of my boots, water rushing past my feet along the river-bed: someone is laughing at me. Eddies swirl in the torrent unable to clear the leaf-clogged drains, and someone is laughing at me.

"Look at this guy," he says, and his companions titter and jeer. "You're being scary, dude. Is that your costume?"

It was Halloween, after all, though I hadn't dressed up. I wore what I usually wear, thrift-store camouflage trousers, a printed shirt from my friend Alley, a maroon-and-blue flannel shirt. No more a disguise than any clothing is.

One of his companions, a gentrifying "woo-girl" (anthropological note: they literally shout "woo" and gentrify everything they touch), sneers at me.

She turns to her friend and says, drunkenly: "Oh my god he's totally on drugs or something." Then she turns back toward me. "You think you're being creepy standing in the rain like that?"

I shake my head. I cannot tell her about the forest we're standing in, the elk crashing through the bramble, the endless dripping of the last-to-fall Maple leaves down upon our heads. I cannot tell her about the river in which I stand.

I smile. "Welcome to Seattle," I say, laughing. "It rains here."

"We're from California," her friend says. I'm disappointed he's such a jerk: he's kinda attractive. "This weather's stupid."

I'm standing in a river. I'm standing in the road, just off the curb. A car passes; I'm surprised to see an auto in the river, the river in front of the gay bar, the gay bar on a night the gates of the dead were thrown wide open, the gates of the sky unhinged as rain soaks everything.

I am in the forest. I am in the city.

II.

Tip some out to the dead, to The Dead who linger forever just behind your eyes, walking alongside your step through puddles and streams over concrete.

Tip some to the dead and notice you're not where you were.

Everyone's bumping into you, pushing against you, surprised for a moment you're there, startled they had gotten so close.

They're drunk, you tell yourself, but not just on vine and grain.

It made no sense to try to tell most people what I was doing for Halloween, so I shrugged when asked. I didn't know myself, really, though I knew I'd walk with the dead.

With grave dirt and an elk tooth and crow feathers in my pocket, I biked to a bar after a shift at my part-time social work job. It was storming, rare for Seattle where the weather is, for 6 months at least, a steady, relentless drip of rain, not a downpour. It had been dry, the earth too compacted to soak up all that water, so streets were flooded, blocked drains overflowed. For that night, at least, the streams and rivers of the Forest-That-Was could run again, un-culverted, upon the surface of the city built over them.

In many urban fantasy novels, there's a spectral, magical city overlain upon the disenchanted mundane. Those writers know a thing or two about magic and a thing or two about cities. But Seattle's not old enough to have a ghost-twin that looks like it, only stranger. Rather, what haunts Seattle in the Other is the Forest-That-Was, the dead forest, the waiting forest.

The dead are not always what has gone before, but also what could have been, what maybe will be. The forest-that-was haunts Seattle, but so too does a second forest; its roots slowly lifting the broken concrete of sidewalks. Plantain, horsetails and chamomile find purchase in the crevices, moss and lichen cover unattended stone. Ferns grow in gutters; aerial moss suspend from uneven brick.

Both the Forest-That-Was and the Forest-That-Will-Be are the same, and they both haunt the city. They co-exist; they merge in the frontage garden, the untended lawn, the volunteer tree. They dance; they collide; they collude in endless war against small-business owners, property developers and civil engineers.

One of my favorite writers, Octavia Butler, was said to be a casualty in this war. Newspapers reporting her death blamed a root-broken sidewalk for a fall that triggered a stroke. But this was propaganda. Later, it came out she had the stroke first and then fell, returning to the forest that seemed to inspire her. Seattle's mayor was unpopular with the propertied classes for leaving sidewalks broken, potholes unfilled—Butler's death was used against him.

Propaganda works like that, though. The first story is the one most remember: The forest killed a famous elderly Black fantasist.

Don't believe such lies.

III.

You weren't from the forest, and now you are, the dark wet places, rain dripping from leaf, mud and rot slicking the paths beneath your feet, your exposed roots.

What are you doing walking when you can stand still, soak deep into the earth, reach like great pillars towards the sky?

The tension between civilisation and nature is a bit obscured in Seattle. From my second-story balcony I see more trees than houses, Crow and Scrubjay, Racoon and Opossum eat the peanuts I leave for them just within arm's reach, and it's easy to forget I'm in a city at all. I've tolerated Seattle most of the last 16 years because of this. Gods know I can't afford to live here, nor afford many of the things that make a city appealing to an artistic queer.

I'm the "degenerate" sort against which Republicans and New-Right anti-civilisationists often complain, lifting a tired screed from the Nazis.

"People like me" move to cities because we honestly like people; we like art; we like culture—all those things you can't find in the suburbs or the rural. I live happiest when I'm among dreams and the people they inhabit.

But I'm also a Druid, a Pagan, an animist. Without raw, breathing Nature, I become parched and eventually wither. The ocean of concrete in strip malls, parking lots and massive highways that comprise the main architectural feature of suburbs, for instance, those feel like murder.

Seattle is unlike most other large American cities in that the forest was never fully obliterated. Though almost every ancient cedar, spruce, red alder and pine was killed to rebuild San Francisco after the fires or to fuel the furnaces of capitalist expansion, or to clear the way for internal migrants from other parts of the United States, Seattle is still a forest.

Though even manufacturing, then war-contracting (Boeing), then an onslaught of businesses completely reliant on near-slave labor and global coal-use (Microsoft, Amazon, Google) have joined the war against the forest here, none have ever conquered the forest.

IV.

You weren't from the forest and now you are, the forest that was before, the ghost-trees and spectral ferns, Elk crashing through bramble, startled by a voice still echoing from the past.

You weren't from the forest but now you will be, awaiting its birth through broken sidewalk and disused alley, hearing it growing through what will soon be your corpse.

You weren't from the forest, but now you can't return here. Wet pavement is river, and you wade through it, unseeing the cars unseeing you.

Pagans make much of the environment, as least romantically. We like the forests and the streams, we idealise the pre-industrial world, worship land-goddesses, divine with symbols from nature. Yet most live in cities or suburbs, drive cars, use computers, work in flourescent-lit offices or stores or restaurants. We like the idea of the forest, but live apart from it, in the urban and suburban–in civilisation.

Civilisation seems to stand against the forest, in the same way that the forest seems to stand against the city. In many critiques of civilisation, the city is the cause of the destruction of the natural world. Some anti-civilisationists, merging the bourgeois anthropology of David Abrams with the misanthropic primitivism of Deep Green Resistance, link almost all the problems of humanity to the birth of cities.

A Kindness of Ravens

On the surface, this appears plausible. As people transitioned to agriculture and settled in one place, the fabric of human society changed. Work was divided, roles ensconced in tradition. Some say the Patriarchy arose first from the urban, men doing one sort of work, women doing another.

Abundance and settlement created surpluses, more than what people could carry with them. Surpluses meant less work, surpluses meant wealth. Surpluses could be stolen; surpluses could be hoarded; surpluses could be extracted. Some say this birthed hierarchy and class.

Gods and ancestors were worshiped in place, not in people. Shrines arose as did temples. Those who tended gods became priests rather than shamans, another division of labor in a settled civility, a class with purpose and power and economic interests. Some say that debt sprung from the need of priests (also skilled scribes) to track donations and the cost of temple labor.

Agriculture, dense living, the need to protect surplus—these, some say, led to population explosions. More people require more resources, need military classes (and conflicts stemming from that need), and need to destroy their environment to extract more resources.

If we extrapolate from what we know now of cities, this story is unassailable. The city seems an illness, a plague, the root of evil, the root of hatred.

This story's eerily too easy, though.

V.

The city's unreal, the forest gates unhinged, and you walk always along the edge, in both worlds and neither.
You are emissary.
You are saboteur.

Is the city then some den of horror, the abode of voracious monsters? Or is it just full of people?

I like people. No, I love them, gods-dammit, even when they jeer me in the rain.

People cluster together. We need each other. We want each other. We love each other. We build off each other, create with each other. What would we do otherwise?

Rugged individualism is a Capitalist lie and will get you killed. Families are great, unless you were born to a developmentally-disabled schizophrenic mother and a violent father. Tribalism is great, if you are in charge and get to choose who is in and who is out. Small villages are fine, if there's at least one person there who you can fall in love with. Degenerates like me don't fare so well in any of those alternatives.

If groups like Deep Green Resistance are correct, the only solution is to destroy the city and all who survive by community, rather than force. And beside, cities are full of queers, trans people, immigrants, Jews, bohemians, libertines—independent folk who threaten those who need small worlds in which to rule.

But the city is undoubtedly sick. The destruction of the environment caused by the urban is undeniable, yet too often denied, even by us "degenerates." The urban professional of today, working at a tech company, progressive of politics, in love with nature? Their organic and free-range foods are produced by immigrants working in near-slave (and sometimes full-slave) conditions. It takes a lot of forest to make toilet paper, a lot of coal to make electricity, a lot of oil to transport food from the farms to the city.

Both the prophets of progress and the prophets of anti-civilisation evoke the pre-historic past. It's either nasty, brutish, and short for the one or Edenic for the other, but both groups are either awfully bad at history or betting that, because no records remain to challenge them, we'll accept their stories without question.

Few dare mention the shorter history, a few hundred years ago. Something arose which turned the endless dance of forest and city into slaughter of one and misery of the other. A great forgetting, an archonic trick, the Demiurge's conquest of Sophia.

Something changed in the world several hundred years ago, something so disastrous, that, like the Holocaust or the nuclear bombings of several Japanese cities, we seem incapable of approaching without shutting down or relying on Nationalist rhetoric.

The world was not always like this. The cities once could never win over the forest. And that wasn't so long ago.

VI.

You are how the forest becomes the city you'll betray.
You are unborn dreaming remembering the past.
You are the endless taking root in the now.

Historian Peter Linebaugh, who has written much about the intersections of 1800's Paganism and anti-Capitalism, suggested that, because the Commons were destroyed by the Cities, the Cities must now become the Commons.

We must say the same thing of the Forests.

This must then be our rallying cry, those who have become 'from the forest' but refuse to accept the notion of mass urban slaughter, like Deep Green Resistance does. In fact, most anti-civilisation rhetoric has become a way of running from the true war, betraying the forest, just as the cult of progress huddles, slump-backed, over backlit screens in self-arousal and vain hope.

The forest-that-was still lives, if you bother to look through the gates on a rainy night in the city. You can be standing, soaked, in front of a gay bar and see the rivers we try to forget. You can even, like I do, chuckle when those who will never see it jeer you.

The forest-that-was lives in the forest-that-will-be, which are both a waiting now, Waltar Benjamin's jetzt-zeit, the pregnant moment, the moment we hold in our hands.

The forest-that-was is also the forest-that-will-be, but only if we let it root through us. It is we who are the mages, the witches, the priests and bards. We are the rogues spreading seeds on the pristine lawns, the saboteurs helping trees lift concrete with their strong roots.

We were from the city. We are now from the forest. And only with our hands can the war finally end and the dance begin anew. The Cities destroy the Forests. The Cities must now become the Forests so that our lives may once again, in the end, nourish the roots of past and future, making the eternal now.

CPSIA information can be obtained
at www.ICGtesting.com
Printed in the USA
BVHW030043080922
646534BV00008B/153